Praise for Journey to Serenity the Companion Book for A Path to Serenity

This is a book to be picked up often, and kept close at hand for those moments when encouragement, and courage, is needed----the author's words of wisdom as well as those of many, many others, well-known and less-known, are myriad. She has lived more adventures and varieties of lifestyles than any person might imagine, much less live. Her leaps into the unknown are awe-inspiring. Her message----Listen to Your Own Message. The eventual establishment of her South Sea Island paradise, aptly named Serenity, brings all of it together, and the fact that it is a success gives its own blessing. Fun, exciting, romantic, emotional, suspenseful and inspiring, all at the same time. Those who read The Journey to Serenity will find many treasures to remember.

—**Richard and Kathy**

This book is your new best friend. It will inspire you to go after that dream you've always wanted no matter what age you may be. Patti has lived an extraordinary life simply by being brave enough to follow her heart.

Beautifully written, the chapters guide you through her journey and gift you with uplifting lessons from a woman who at almost 80 still runs the resort she built on an island in Tonga.

If you've ever been afraid of leaving a situation that no longer serves you, please read this book. You will see yourself in these pages, and Patti's advice will give you the courage to finally discover who you were meant to be.

—**Erin L. Matlock**

A wonderul, inspiring book filled with wisdom, stories and encouragement to remind you that you are never too old to experience adventure and follow new passions or interests. Patti is amazing! I have recommended it to others and am purchasing it as gifts.

—**Melissa Wolak MS CCC-SLP**

Read this book cover to cover in about an hour. It was extremely empowering. I've bookmarked certain pages for future reflection.

I'll be sending it to my stepdaughter this week in the hopes that it will help her get through some challenging times that she's currently experiencing.

Thank you, Patti, for sharing your journey to serenity with all of us.

—**KIM**

I really loved reading this book. It is empowering for all women, especially women over 50. It gave me the insight that life is not over at 50, but the second (best) chapter is only beginning. Make your own choices! This book is an easy to read story about a woman who made these choices after 50 with strength, courage and faith.

—**Maria de Rooij**

Loved this book. Great inspiration for any age but especially someone in there 40's, 50's or 60's who thinks they are too late to do something they have always wanted to do. Patti shows with her own life that it is never ever too late and she is living proof. A great read to give you the kick you need to get on and do that thing you have always dreamt of.

—**t woodcock**

Journey to Serenity is a wonderful book, I devoured it in a day. Patti Ernst generously shares her brave journey and the lessons learned along the way. The book is filled with warmth and wisdom and will inspire you to look at life differently. Thank you Patti !!

—**Anita**

A Path to Serenity

Leading with Your Heart
and
Living Simply

Patti Ernst

Copyright © 2021 Patti Ernst.

Published by *Lead With Your Heart Press*

ALL RIGHTS RESERVED. This book contains material protected under International and Federal Copyright Laws and Treaties. Any unauthorized reprint or use of this material is prohibited. No part of this book may be reproduced or transmitted in any form or by any means, electronic or mechanical, including photocopying, recording, or by any information storage and retrieval system without express written permission from the author/publisher.

The content of this book is not intended to be a substitute for professional medical advice, diagnosis, or treatment. Always seek the advice of your physician or other qualified health provider with any questions you may have regarding a medical or mental health condition.

ISBN: 978-1-64184-568-7 (Paperback)

A Companion Workbook for Journey to Serenity

To help you relax, contemplate, and think about life in balance, making changes and living simply.

If it is to be it is up to me!!!   *Little Words* = Big Idea

Dedicated to:

*Pioneers of consciousness willing to:
lead with their hearts, choose love not fear, change their
lives, and change the world.*

Table of Contents

Prologue xiii

Part One
Who Am I? A short exploration of where I am *now*. 3

Part Two
Who We Are is Based On 17
Let's Explore these Areas with a Bit of Writing. 21
My View of the Earth and My Place On It 21
Consciousness. 28
Beliefs 38
Power To... 45
Understanding the Mind/Body/Spirit Connection 51

Part Three
Nurturing and Nourishing My Earth Suit. 59
Self-Awareness. 62
Life in Balance. 71
The Power of Breath 77
Our Energy Systems 83

Movement and Exercise for Body/Mind/Spirit 89
Nourishment for Body/Mind/Spirit 95
Meditative Practices: Mindfulness, Yoga, Qigong 104
Work/Play/Sleep 116
Re-Creation through Recreation 121
Becoming: Who Am I Now? Who Am I Becoming? 128

Epilogue 135
Lights in the Darkness. 141
    Quotes from Giants. 141
Guiding Lights 145
    A list of books, Podcasts, Videos 145
About the Author 149

Prologue

*The minute you begin to do what you really want to do,
it's a different kind of life.*
R. Buckminster Fuller

Six miles of white sand beach and I am here alone. When the season starts there will be many, but probably no more than thirty at a time, spread along the pristine beaches, exploring the rain forest, enjoying the crystal clear water, or traveling on the sea. We all come to this isolated place to reconnect with nature and our essential beings. We are blessed.

I came to this island and built a resort almost fourteen years ago, after a ten-year journey. My first book, *Journey to Serenity: Strength – Courage – Faith*, tells that story. *A Path to Serenity* is a companion workbook: a remembrance of specific challenges and how I faced them along my way. There are techniques I used to clear my mind, let go of old beliefs, emotions, habits, and patterns of behavior, as well as to keep myself strong and healthy as I moved through the discovery and re-inventing process.

When I wrote *Journey to Serenity* it was to help those who felt the call to change their life. Recently, I realized that the wisdom of many is needed to solve the problems of today's world. Some people are happy and living their dreams. They are not needing to change. Others feel something is missing. This book is for those who sense there is more for them to do during this lifetime but are unsure how to get there. It is my hope that you will use this book as an inspiration to find *your own* path to serenity, your heart, and your purpose. It is a path we must travel if we are to make changes in our lives and in the world. If we do not wake up and change things, we face a bleak future. We all have the ability to live from our heart with strength, courage, and faith. We must take the opportunity, and do it.

My journey was long, gentle, and spread out over many years. You may not have that luxury. Change does not need to take a long time. I took years to search for my giants/heroes before I was brave enough to set out on my own "hero's journey." I continued to read, travel, think, sit in silence, and experience. I grew, changed, and slowly opened. Starting with little guidance or experience I found both along the way.

The world is different now. There are many more "giants" – ordinary people writing, speaking, teaching, and inspiring others. There are people who have listened, thought deeply, and developed classes with plans to follow. This book is not meant to be the only guide, but to suggest places you can find specific help that might be encouraging to you as you journey to a new stronger you.

Many people are awakening or have awakened. Yet, at the same time, many are being mesmerized into a deep sleep – a seductive place of comfort where they don't question what is happening. In some cases people have given away their power and allowed themselves to be programmed by television, videos, news, social media, and the special interests of a few, at the expense of the enrichment of many. Some live to obtain the feeling of security, rather than living fearlessly, using their voice and power to create the life they are meant to live – their purpose.

One gift I possess is that I am old enough to remember a different world. A world we have almost lost. I have been on this planet almost eighty years. When I was younger, life seemed simple and easy. We grew our own food, kept our money at the bank on the corner, walked to school and church. In my early adult years we faced huge challenges and energetically made changes. It feels like it is time to look at the world with great discernment and do that again.

Long ago in a video series by Bill Moyers and Joseph Campbell, *The Power of Myth*, I heard the words of Chief Seattle. "Whatever befalls the Earth – befalls the sons of the Earth. Man did not weave the web of life – he is merely a strand in it. Whatever he does to the web, he does to himself. When the secret corners of the forest are heavy with scent of many men, when the view of the ripe hills is blotted by talking wires… the end of living and the beginning of survival." In many ways that is where we are now. It is time to turn things around.

Recently Brent BecVar, of the Chopra Center, taught a class in which he said, it is as though the universe took on the role of a parent and said to us, "Go to your rooms and stay there and think about what you have done." Because of a virus, we have all been sent to our rooms. May we finally take the time to think about what has been happening, the mindless way we have been rushing around, using resources, and giving away our personal freedoms. Can we use this experience wisely? Can we retreat into silence and think deeply until we see a way to turn things around?

I believe in us. We are a magnificent species. We have been moving at such a pace that we haven't had time to sit and think deeply about what is happening in our world. It is time to do that. Climate change, the need for civil rights for all people, and the need for compassion, are demanding our attention.

Living almost alone in the woods, I feel what life used to be like. I now realize, I am living much like indigenous people used to live. Isolated from society and the need to rush, I have time to fully appreciate the closeness I have with the beauty and healing power of nature and to observe what's happening in the world. Time to think about what might be done to reclaim our gentle strength, compassion, and caring.

Henry David Thoreau chose to spend time in isolation on Walden Pond. He said, "Most men lead lives of quiet desperation and go to the grave with their song still in them." He also said, "Go confidently in the direction of your dreams. Live the life you have imagined." And one more thing, "Not until we are completely lost or turned around… do we begin to find ourselves." After living in the woods and on the ocean for so many years in such isolation, I find myself with a true appreciation of his words.

Can we redefine our journey? Can we reinvent ourselves, our culture, and our society? Can we finally realize what an amazing planet our home is and how blessed we are to be living here? Can we fully appreciate those with whom we share the earth? Can we understand the mistakes that have been made and learn from them? Can we change?

Many of us feel we are in a state of chaos. That is where we are meant be. In order to move from one state of being and enter a significantly different state of being, we must pass through a time of chaos. It is a time when old outmoded ways and systems can break down and give way to new creations.

I liken it to the caterpillar that eats its way destructively through its environment and has no idea of what the future holds. Inside the chrysalis it changes dramatically. That stage is a necessary stage of chaos when it breaks down and gives way to the new creation. When the process is complete the butterfly emerges. There is a timing to this that cannot be rushed. We are in that transition. In the process, we must cherish our humanity and freedom to choose. We must face this change with deep thought and heartfelt responsibility.

I offer this as a guide to help you design your own "path with heart" to an essential place of serenity, calm, and strength. It is a roadmap, *if needed*, to guide you to the questions you might ask, as well as the steps and processes you may consider. Be curious. Ask why, ask what, ask and *listen*. Discovering and embracing our whys helps us become wise. Knowledge is important. Imagination is even more so, but wisdom must be at the core of what we do, where we go, and how we think and behave.

The door is open. The opportunity is now, to guide us home to who we are and what we have come here to contribute. Every single one of us has something to share. Listening, getting self-importance out of the way, and coming from a place of gratitude and service, puts us in the right vibration to move forward.

Write to discover what you know and what you need to learn. If you're not used to writing, use Julia Cameron's book, *The Artists Way*, to help you get started. It is about releasing blocks, limiting beliefs, deprecating thoughts, and creating the life you are meant to live. My intention is that you will use *this* book to move from where you are – possibly a place of discomfort, stagnation, and anxiety – to a place of inspiration, enthusiasm, and newfound energy. When you are living from your heart, the place of courage, passion, and purpose, your life will have more meaning, focus, energy, and joy.

May this be a joyful journey as you plan and discover your path to a re-created, reinvented, self and to a powerful, more conscious life. We can live mindlessly. We can allow our individual freedoms to be eroded. We can destroy this amazing planet and the many forms of life on it or we can turn ourselves around and save our lives, the lives of those with whom we share the earth, and our precious home. We can't continue to say, "Someone should do something." We are those "someones," those brilliant beings who have a reason to be here. We need to accept that responsibility, support each other, and help make needed changes. The journey ahead will take courage and massive amounts of heart and love. The words of Buckminster Fuller are encouraging. "We are called to be architects of the future, not it's victims… I am not trying to council any of you to do anything really special except dare to think, dare to go with the truth, and dare to really love completely." It is time to heed his words.

We must take time to just "be," to sit in silence, and listen until we find the serenity, peace, and clarity that will help us know where we are meant to put our energy. We do not need to overthrow the old ways, but we can focus on the positive and create something better than we have. If we learn to care for our bodies and minds we can stay healthy and strong during this process. Remember, it wasn't the hare that won the race! Slow and steady, with wisdom and grace, can return us to a magnificent place.

I have a life-long habit of scanning and going to the end of a book, first, to see where it is taking me. When I wrote this book, I added a description of the journey that you might embrace. When deciding where to put it, I chose the last chapter, *Becoming*. If you want to know where this is heading, I encourage you to briefly take a look at the last chapter first, and then return here to start on the path. Crazy, but it works for me!

With love, support, and appreciation,

Patti

Part One

Who Am I?

This may be the most important question we will ever ask ourselves, and one to which many give very little conscious thought. This book is designed to help you contemplate and formulate your answers to this question. It is about awareness and self-care in the 21st century.

In the book, *Tying Rocks to Clouds,* when asked "What is the purpose of life?" the Dalai Lama answered with one memorable word. "Happiness." The Buddha said attachments cause suffering. Letting go of attachments, emotional and physical, can help us move towards happiness. Jesus came to give us an important message, "Love one another." This implies be kind to one another, support, help, encourage, care for, listen to, respect, and appreciate one another. That certainly will lead to a happier world. Bahaullah, founder of the Baha'i faith, said, "We are all one." Unity and equality are his messages. "We are drops of one ocean, we are leaves of one tree." Victor Frankel named his book *Man's Search for Meaning,* and says the most important task in a person's life is finding purpose and meaning, and living with that at our core.

In order to change and move from where we are to where we desire to be, we need to go through a process. We must think of what we appreciate about ourselves and our situation, what needs to change, and the resources we possess to make those changes. We need to consider how our beliefs, health, resilience, strength, courage, and faith will either support or inhibit that journey. To accomplish this, some require silence and isolation. Others process better when they ride a bike, walk, climb a mountain, dance, or get together with friends of like mind. Self-exploration will help us uncover our own path. We all have different needs and different journeys.

In the following sections, we will explore and contemplate the answers to many questions:

Who Am I? Why am I here? How am I using this gift of a lifetime I have been given? Am I who my parents, teachers, community, or friends told me I should be? Am I who I have chosen to become, based on guidance, inner awareness, and personal choice? What do I love doing? What drains my energy? What inspires me?

Self-exploration helps us uncover our path, our awareness, and our way forward. Here are some questions to help you discover who you are *now*. In the next sections you will explore and contemplate who you are *becoming*. If you find thinking doesn't bring the answers, breathe deeply, get quiet, and wait for the answers to come. Go into the silence. If we always try to figure things out, we deny ourselves the power of just allowing the answers to come. Use this book to inspire contemplation, meditation, as well as thinking.

When you finish this book come back to this section and see if your answers have changed.

Use seven or more words to describe who you are now.

Circle the virtues/values that guide your life. Find more on the Internet and add to the list:
love, joy, peace, courage, strength, patience, kindness, gentleness, generosity, compassion, adventure, achievement, curiosity, authenticity, honesty, bravery, perseverance, commitment, confidence, wisdom, humility, faith, ...

On the next page create a timeline.
Use five to ten major events in your life – turning points – that brought you to where you are today. If you wish, engage your imagination and extend the timeline into the future. Use the page following the timeline to write about what you discover. Notice patterns, preferences, strengths, talents, skills, interests, habits, ...

PATTI ERNST

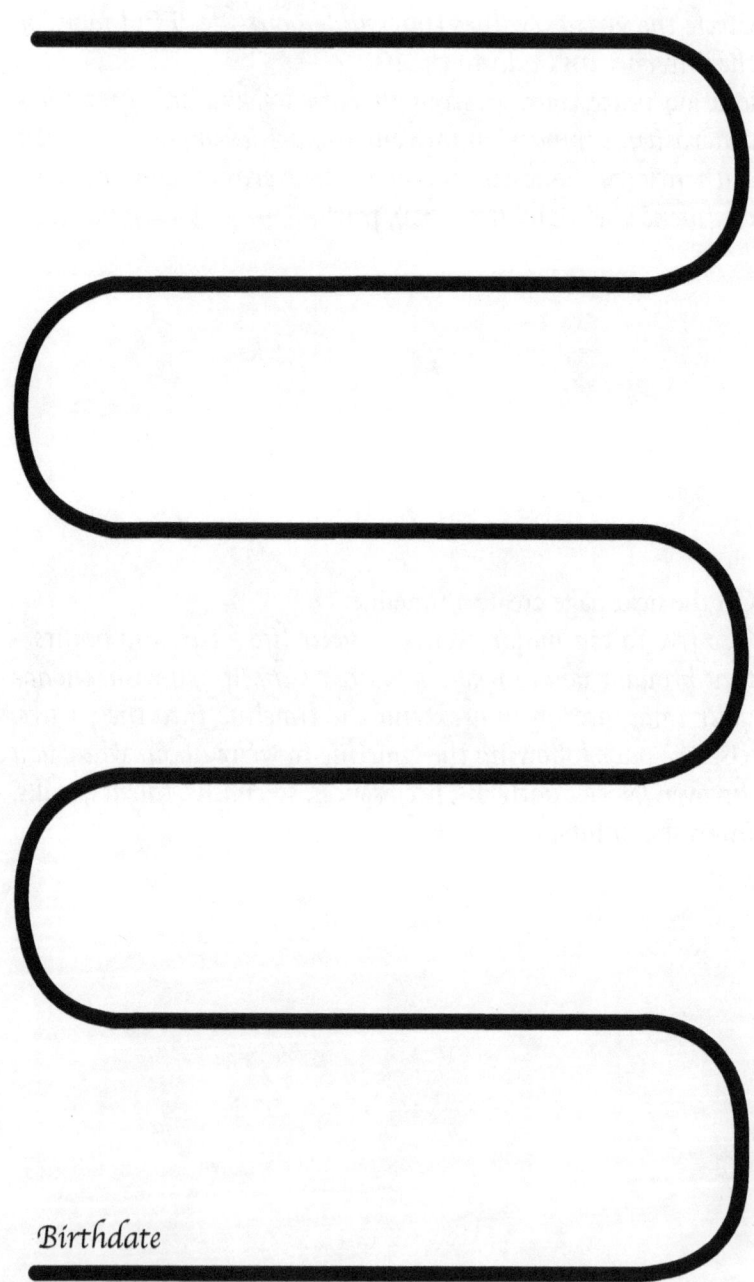

Birthdate

PATH TO SERENITY

What makes you happy about who and where you are? What do you love about your life? What are you good at? What things do you appreciate and value about yourself in this moment?

In what ways do you wish you were different, or your life was different?

Are you happy moving forward in the same direction or are you ready for a change?

What things need to be changed?

What must you sacrifice, or risk (things or ideas), in order to change? Risk and sacrifice are not synonymous with loss.

What choices are available to you now?

Remember: *We always have a choice! There will be consequences for the choices we make or don't make. Which consequences are you willing to live with?*

What are your goals for the present?

What are your goals for five years from now?

What are your goals for ten years from now?

What are your lifetime goals? Are there others who have achieved similar goals, others you admire and wish you could emulate? Have you heard their story? Have you learned from their example?

What are the gifts and talents you have been given, that if nurtured, strengthened, and developed, might help you, those you know, or humanity?

PATH TO SERENITY

Which of your goals makes your heart sing or inspires action? What brings you joy?

For what purpose are you on this planet?

Part Two

Who We Are is Based On ...

Our View of the Earth and Our Place on It

We live on a beautiful planet in the solar system of one star. We are part of a vast universe (one song) filled with many other stars and star systems. Einstein believed we are part of a vast network he called the field. Today, physicists are proving the existence of such a unified field. We share this planet with an incredible number of amazing living beings.

We are an evolving species. Humans, two hundred or two thousand years ago, were not aware of the capabilities we now possess. We are capable of more than most of us have ever imagined. Barbara Marx Hubbard said we have been in an embryonic stage of development and are now moving forward into the childhood of humanity. Are we caring for each other or fighting with each other? What are we capable of if we focus on cooperation and the positive, rather than "survival of the fittest" and the negative?

Our bodies are made up of trillions of cells that must work together, cooperatively, to keep us healthy and functioning well. We have based our society on the interpretation of the work of Charles Darwin that says it is the "survival of the fittest" that keeps us well and evolving. Many now believe that what will save us is embracing the way the cells that make up our bodies function. Survival of the most cooperative and most able to work together for the good of the whole, is what supports our body, and will support life on this planet.

Our Consciousness

We are pioneers of consciousness. In the past, adventurers explored uncharted lands. Today we are exploring human consciousness. Of what are humans capable? Are we using our full potential? How does our inner world affect our outer word? It has been said, "Go within or go without." What understandings can we develop that will benefit ourselves and humanity?

Our Beliefs

Our choices and actions are based on our beliefs – positive or negative. Are your beliefs valid or outdated? Were they handed down from parents, society, another time in life, or another place in the world? We must let go of beliefs that no longer serve us and strengthen those that do. Henry Ford said, *"Believe you can or believe you can't – either way you'll be right."*

Our Power To....

Today power is beginning to mean, "power to," not "power over" as it did in the past. We are far more capable and powerful than most of us realize. Margaret Mead said, "Never doubt the ability of a small group of committed people to change the world. It is the only thing that ever has." We have the power to create through our thoughts. What are our thoughts creating? What are we using our power to do? Yes, there are those in the world that want to remain in a system of "power over", but we are beginning to understand there is a choice. It is time to choose the power of love rather than the love of power.

Pushing against the river or paddling up stream can lead to unconscious thinking and stress. It is better to turn our boat around and go with the flow, listening for guidance, and creating new ways of changing with gentle strength. Buckminster Fuller stated, "You never change things by fighting the existing reality. To change something, build a new model that makes the existing model obsolete." Staying focused intently in the present moment, the only place we have power, helps us to *influence* the future as it unfolds. My favorite song from Pippin starts, "Rivers belong where they can ramble, Eagles belong where they can fly…" In the middle of the song these words have always inspired me. "Somehow I want my life to be something more than long." We have the power to create the life of our heart's desire and to be of service to others as we help to change the world by using gentle strength, courage, and faith.

Our Understanding of the Body/Mind/Spirit Connection

Before the turn of the century, Herb Benson and Joan Borysenko created the mind/body clinic at Harvard University. The work they did helped us to see the body/mind as one system. Our beliefs and the thoughts we think affect the choices we make and the actions we take that create who we are physically, emotionally, and spiritually. The mental *choice* to eat nutrient dense food that provides energy and to exercise regularly will keep our body strong and flexible longer.

The Okinawa Program, by Wilcox and Wilcox is a book that looks closely at a society of people that have lived consciously for a long time. They eat well, exercise, have good social connections, and are spiritually awake. The people who have lived this way are strong and healthy until the age of 120. The most important factor, in my opinion, is their *belief* that they are children *until age fifty*. At that point they *enter adulthood* and at *ninety-five they enter old age* gracefully with much celebration. They have the respect of their community, which takes great pride in their strength, and benefits from the wisdom they have acquired over many years and share freely.

Our thoughts affect our body, or as Carolyn Myss says in *Anatomy of the Spirit*, "Your biography… becomes your biology."

Let's Explore these Areas with a Bit of Writing

My View of the Earth and My Place On It

> "Angels can fly
> because they can take themselves lightly."
> G.K. Chesterson

For centuries humankind has changed gradually. The last one hundred years has brought enormous growth. Some changes have been supportive and helpful – some detrimental. Currently, we are moving at an even greater pace. We are developing more consciousness and awareness. We now recognize our ability to create our reality through our thoughts, positive or negative, as well as the importance of focusing on what we *choose* to create. These are not new ideas, but recently greater numbers of people have acquired these understandings. Physics, more than biology, is influencing our view of the way the body functions. The concept of the field, sound, light, and vibration influences our perception of the way the body works.

Are we leading a sustainable existence? Buckminster Fuller said, in *Operating Manual for Spaceship Earth;* "We have everything we need to support all of us on this spaceship which travels a huge distance around the sun every year." The question is: Are we using these resources wisely and distributing them well? Are we being conscious of the needs of *all* those with whom we share this planet, or is a small minority, who value things we do not, leading the way?

This year, I heard John Perkins speak on a podcast. He talked about his book, *Touching the Jaguar: Transforming Fear into Action to Change Your Life and the World*. Midway through a very lucrative career he found himself realizing he was serving the need for profit of a wealthy few, at the expensive of large groups of indigenous people. With much soul-searching, risk, and effort he turned his life around and is now making a significant difference in the world.

This amazing book touched my heart and lead me to another book by a friend of his, Lynn Twist. In *The Soul of Money* she asks, are we embracing scarcity or sufficiency as the basic principle of our economy? Are we are creating a "*me and you*" society or a "*me or you*" society?" She encourages us to understand when we have "*enough,*" using this as a guideline for conscious living. Having spent much time with the indigenous people in South America, she explains how greed and the desire for profit, in the endless search for oil, lumber, and soil to use for farming, is causing the destruction of the rain forest, as well as sacred lands around the world.

Pointing out how we desire more and more and thinking that is what will make us happy, she suggests it is not the thing we desire but the *feeling* we get when we acquire it. For example, we may think if we get a new car it will make us happy. If our old car is good enough, can we find something else that will fulfill our need for that sort of happiness, and use our resources for something more essential? Her book challenges us to think about money in a new sustainable way that focuses less on consumption and more on responsible choices that will benefit the world. Tom Shadyak's movie, *I Am*, gives us a very similar message about over consumption.

Are we remembering the old saying that says what we give out into the world is returned to us tenfold? This works well if what we are giving out is love, kindness, caring, generosity, and support. However, if we are sending out anger, hatred, selfishness, greed, as well as ignoring the pain of others, that is what we will reap.

Now, take time to contemplate these questions. If you cannot think of answers, allow your mind to be still and listen for answers to come.

List some major changes in humanity, technology, or our way of life, and how they have affected our quality-of-life:

During my lifetime.

During the last one hundred years.

During the last one thousand years.

What positive or negative changes can I imagine for the future?

During the next ten years.

During the next one hundred years.

During the next one thousand years.

How can I, as an individual, influence the direction we are moving?

Buckminster Fuller came to a major turning point and contemplated suicide at a devastating time in his life. He picked himself up, turned himself around, and set a goal to see what one man could do, in his lifetime, to make a difference in the world. At midlife he became a prolific inventor, philosopher, and a much sought after speaker at universities around the world. He said, "Never forget you are one-of-a-kind. No matter how overwhelming life's challenges and problems seem to be, one person can make a difference in the world. In fact, it is always because of one person that all the change that matters in the world comes about. So be that one person."

What could I do with the time and talents I have, or am able to develop, to make a difference in the world? If you feel too small to make a difference, it has been suggested you try sleeping with a mosquito for one night.

What is the meaning or purpose that directs my life?

What are some beliefs, positive or negative, that got humankind to the place we are now?

What big ideas or beliefs have led me to become who I am?

What big ideas/beliefs can help, or hinder, humankind or me as we develop, change, and move into the future?

Help:

Hinder:

Consciousness

The greatest thing in the world is not so much where we are but in what direction we are moving.
Oliver Wendell Holmes

Sitting on the beach under the stars reminds me of the years I spent sailing – two and a half years from Tonga to Bali. One of the amazing things I saw on my many all-night watches were iridescent dolphins swimming alongside the boat. The plankton was activated by motion and as the dolphins swam past, tiny lights outlined their bodies.

Now, walking through the rainforest and seeing the vines traveling up the trees, I notice how thick and large they are at their base and how thin and strong they become high in the branches of other trees. As I walk through the forest at night, listening to the insects, I notice the way the full moon lights up the leaves and branches of the trees and creates moon shadows on the forest floor. This is the wealth I appreciate and wish to share with humanity.

Nature has always evoked a sense of gratitude in me. I remember as a child enjoying fireflies. Where did they go? I heard a statistic recently that shocked and saddened me. It is said we have lost eighty percent of the insects and seventy percent of the songbirds that used to exist. What is happening to our precious planet as we embrace "progress" and build more and more cities and roads? I walk along the beach and see the crystal clear water and wonder how many people experience these things? Many never do, and we are poorer for it.

I have learned it is from a place of serenity that I can more effectively face problems, respond, create, and solve them. When we snorkel, we cannot go if there has been a storm and the water is churned up and full of sand. If we do, we see nothing. We must wait until it settles and clears.

We need clarity. Clarity comes when we spend time in silence, serenity, and calm. This is a wonderful reminder I heard during the last year, "Calm is a Superpower." As "pioneers of consciousness," we are developing greater awareness and are capable of more than ever. The question is, are we developing our capabilities and using them wisely and responsibly? Are we being discerning? Are we aware of what's happening in the world? Can we sense an increase in the freedom we have or is our freedom eroding? Are we in control of our decisions or are we being increasingly controlled?

Now is the time to use our insight, imagination, and strength to build a world based on compassion, caring, integrity, and vision. To gather around a campfire and share our visions rather than sit in front of a television (tell a vision) and be told a vision. Do we have the courage to move from pain to purpose, from aggression to compassion, from hating to helping? Can we see with 20/20 vision, the mistakes we've made, correct them, and move toward who we are meant to be? It is time to slow down, act mindfully, allow our consciousness to expand, our hearts to open, and our "little lights" to shine.

How am I more conscious, aware, and discerning than I was five, or twenty-five years ago? What do I know now that I did not know then?

In what ways have I expanded my capabilities physically, mentally, emotionally, and spiritually?

In what additional ways can I expand them now, and how will that benefit me?

How can I become more aware and live mindfully?

Do I see problems as troubles? Do I see them as challenges and opportunities to grow, learn, and change for the better? Buddhists say, "Another problem, another opportunity to grow." Reframe one current problem you have, as an opportunity. Then try two more.

What negative thoughts are limiting me now? Take time to observe the effects negative thoughts have on me.

What positive thoughts are encouraging and inspiring me now? Take time to observe the energizing power of positive thoughts when trying to accomplish something.

A Technique That Might Help When I am Ready to Change

Respond vs. React

Human behavior takes the path of least resistance. Often we react unconsciously the same way over and over again. Like a river flowing down a hill, the course, the path of least resistance, is set unless something purposefully changes it. Ask yourself: Am I reacting the same way over and over rather than responding consciously? What can I do to change the automatic reactions I have in some situations?

Try this to help with conscious change. When something happens that upsets you:

1 - Press Pause
2 - Breathe Deeply
3 - Take Time to Think and Feel Your Emotions
4 - Then Respond Consciously

This takes awareness. We must do something that will break the old limiting patterns. We can change the neural pathways in our brain that use the path of least resistance and create a reaction. To create a new nerve connection, neural pathway, we must reward that pattern every time we respond consciously. If you need help with this, you can go to a therapist trained in NLP, Neural Linguistic Programming. In the next paragraph, is a simple process to try on your own. It may take a while but it is worth your time to change an unconscious, unproductive, or unwanted habit.

The STICA Technique

Stop: Press your Pause button.
Think: Ask yourself, "Do I want to react in the same old way or respond consciously?"
Inhale: Inhale deeply through your nose and slowly exhale through your mouth, as many times as you need to change your emotional state.
Choose: Make a choice to try a new way.
Act: Respond consciously!

Now give yourself a "STICA" for a job well done. Stop and acknowledge your success. Give yourself a small reward. Remember to take time to notice and celebrate your successes. Keep a record of your wins in all areas of your life. This will help you remember your progress and provide an opportunity to express gratitude for what you've achieved. Gratitude is a powerful tool.

While you are practicing, remember these 3 P's:

Pause   Patience   Persistence

List five goals I have for the present, the next few years, or my lifetime?

Mind Map

On the next page create a mind map for one of your goals. Start by putting your goal in a circle or cloud shape in the center of the page. From there, draw branches out to circles in which you write the big tasks that will help you reach your goal. Use single words or short phrases to fill in the circles. From each of those circles/major tasks, draw branches that will lead to the small jobs that make up the larger tasks. Once complete, you can begin by prioritizing and starting on some of the smaller jobs on the outer edges of the map. That will lead you to complete the bigger tasks. When those are all complete you will have reached your goal. A mind map is an excellent way to get things out of your brain and onto paper. You don't have to write things in a particular order. Just allow them to flow out onto the paper creating order later. Then start with the easiest jobs and slowly move toward the larger tasks that will eventually lead to completion of your goal.

PATTI ERNST

PATH TO SERENITY

Beliefs

We are powerful beings.
We have the power to celebrate who we are or change.
This power comes from the beliefs and values we have, the thoughts we choose to think based on those beliefs and values, the choices we choose to make based on those thoughts, and the actions we take based on those choices.

Beliefs create our thoughts, attitudes, choices, and behavior. Am I who others expect me to be? Am I who I have chosen to become based on inner awareness, personal experience, growth, and choice?

Our beliefs and thoughts are what direct our lives. Beliefs are creating not only our lives but are shaping our civilization, and have been for centuries. We are beginning to understand that some of the beliefs we have been embracing are incorrect. They come from an outmoded view of the world based on what we believed were scientific facts or social truths. Some have now been proved outdated, inaccurate, or misleading.

Seeing the world through the lens of Quantum Physics gives us a very different picture than through the lens of Newtonian Science. By clearing the myths of old beliefs, we see ourselves as powerful beings that have the ability to create our world through our thoughts, rather than as victims living in a fear-based world.

Bruce Lipton, in *The Biology of Belief*, and many of his other teachings, gives us detailed insight into what is actually happening in our world. He says lack of knowledge leads to lack of power. For a long time we have thought our genes controlled our lives. Now, we understand that our consciousness, what we eat, how much we exercise, and our environment are actually what controls our genes. Our genes are just a blueprint. Our environment and our choices are the architect. The Human Genome Project (HGP) that took place from 1990 to 2003, proved we are not victims of our genetics, as we believed in the past. That is a belief we must change.

We have beliefs that support us, as well as limiting beliefs. I have a limiting belief that I am working on now. As a child, in church, I remember hearing, "*It is harder for a rich man to get into heaven than for a camel to go through the eye of the needle.*" This belief has had a huge impact on me. I am using a variety of methods to overcome this.

Another belief that supports me is, "*If I don't feel abundant today, with what I have, I will never feel abundant, no matter how much I have.*" It is amazing how the beliefs we take on in childhood or the ones we acquire as we grow and in adulthood have such a deep effect. They become part of our subconscious programming, and the subconscious controls 95% of our behavior. If we desire to make a change we must find a way to get into the subconscious and change the programming. Psych-K, explained in the book, *The Missing Piece/Peace in Your Life* by Robert M Williams and EFT, Emotional Freedom Technique, referred to as "tapping", are two methods that can be used to access the subconscious. *The Tapping Solution* by Nick Ortner, is another good resource.

Let's explore beliefs.

1- Write down your beliefs in the categories starting on the next page (add more, or replace some, if you wish).

2- Think about each one and mark it with a letter. Where did it come from?

    F = Family
    S = Society
    C = Conscious Thought and Choice

3- Spend time with these beliefs: reflect, evaluate, and mark with three different symbols.

    & = This belief serves, strengthens, and supports me. Celebrate and reinforce it.

    # = This belief no longer serves me. It is a limiting belief. Release, rewrite, or change it.

    ? = This belief needs more thought. Take time to reflect. Make a conscious decision.

My Beliefs About

Myself

God

Family

Money

Responsibility

Humanity

Love

Work

Play

Exercise

Health

Relationships/Friends

Power To...

If not me, who? And if not now, when?
Mikhail Gorbachev

Today, for some, power means, "power to," not "power over" as it has for so long. There are still those in the world who want power over, but that is slowly changing as we wake up. As we grow and change we begin to realize how powerful we are. Each of us came to this planet for a purpose. If we all would stop, get silent, listen, recognize, and embrace that purpose, we could use the power we have to create needed change in our lives and in the world. Take time to discover your purpose, mission, and dreams. Then apply your power to achieve your goals.

During my journey to serenity I used my power to change my life, to find my purpose, strength, courage, and faith. I traveled, grew, and built a resort in the South Pacific where people come to get back to nature and the essence of who they truly are.

Here are some people that have helped me recently to increase my power. I have been using it for years, but these teachers have given more depth to my understanding. All of them have books, YouTube videos, or online classes that are powerful resources for change. There you can experience their teachings firsthand. I am always finding new teachers and new inspiration.

I am currently reading a book by Sir Ken Robinson called, *The Element*. So many people enjoyed the book that he wrote *Finding Your Element* to help support their process. It is an outstanding book in which he says, " The element is when natural aptitude meets personal passion." He encourages people to go on a Quest, a journey of intention, but you are not sure what you are looking for. He likens it to the "Hero's Journey" described so well by Joseph Campbell. I feel the hero's journey was a big part of my process. Both men encourage people to pursue what truly inspires them, to "follow their bliss," and doors will open where they didn't even know there were doors.

Foster and Kimberly Carter Gamble produced a film called *Thrive* many years ago. It is still very current and available on YouTube. It is filled with information about how physics, the field, and our social systems work. They just released another film, *Thrive II*, which focuses on alternative energy systems and ways to function within our social systems. The films highlight people who are using their power to achieve major goals. Both videos are well worth taking the time to watch.

In the last few weeks, I have come across the work of Price Prichard. His book, You^2, validates my experiences. He says working harder and struggling isn't always the answer. Yes, you must explore and find your passion, purpose, and goals. However, with a specific goal in total focus, you must imagine the end result. When you make a decision and commitment, you cut off other possibilities. Then, it is essential for you to move with clear vision, intense emotion, and passion. Learn from your mistakes and completely trust the outcome. Act when opportunities arise, not waiting until you are ready. In this way you will reach your goal efficiently and effectively.

Joe Dispenza confirms this. His advice is to rehearse your future with feeling. It is strong emotion that gives your desire the power it needs to come into reality. He says to look inward and merge your consciousness with greater consciousness. That is the meaning of the mantra at the beginning of my daily yoga practice. The Sanskrit words mean, may my finite consciousness connect with infinite consciousness. He says you must feel "empowered before you reach success, feel abundance before you gain wealth, and feel whole before you are healed." For example, as I planned and gathered the materials to create the resort, I had a clear vision and my joy, enthusiasm, and elevated emotions moved it to completion.

Both Joe and his friend Gregg Braden, who wrote *Human by Design*, *The Divine Matrix* and many other important books, reminds us to acknowledge every success. We must give thanks even before our prayer is answered, and feel success before completion. Gregg says we are powerful beings who need to gather information, have experiences, and take charge of our wellbeing. When we have questions, if we ask from a coherent heart space, the heart will answer more quickly and accurately than the brain. It is only recently that we have come to understand the full power of the heart. Heart-brain coherence is explained in a later section. Gregg is passionate about helping us understand how amazing we are as humans, before we give away control to artificial intelligence systems that are emerging swiftly and could affect us profoundly.

The *Untethered Soul* and *The Surrender Experiment* by Michael Singer came to my attention this spring. He says, "The mind can be a dangerous place to be, as well as a gift." It can be extremely critical by putting us down, bullying us, and telling us we're too fat, no one likes us, we will never amount to anything, … He suggests meditation to help us to gain control of a bullying mind. Much of his life was spent with an awareness of how the mind can destroy self-confidence, block access to our intuition, and progress toward our goals. He tells how he isolated himself and used meditation to gain better control of his unruly mind, which then brought him amazing success.

Barbara Marx Hubbard encourages us to regularly listen to our intuition, that still small voice within. We can simply ask and listen carefully. She says to keep a journal in which we write questions and then wait for the answers to come. After that, it is essential to use our power to follow this guidance as it "comes from the growing edge of evolution." At a difficult time in her life, when she felt unfulfilled and needed to change, she was introduced to Abraham Maslow who became her mentor. He told her, "All self-actualizing people have one thing in common – chosen work they find intrinsically self-rewarding and of service to others – a unique vocation that gives them pleasure. They are rewarded in the doing of their work." I think of the many times I left a full day of massage feeling, I cannot believe I'm being paid for doing this joyful work.

Kelly Brogan, in *Own Your Self*, writes about her journey from being a prescription-writing psychiatrist in New York City, to leaving her practice and opening a new one based on the belief that we can heal on our own. She believes we can attain mental health naturally, with the support of a doctor who understands how to guide us to embrace proper diet, activity, and habits of thought that support the body's ability to heal itself. She talks about the dark night of the soul, which we will experience many times on our "hero's journey." She says a dark night is like a cloud covering the sun. There are times when you no longer know who you are, because "the false self is crumbling" and making way for the authentic self. She says, "It is never too late to drop the mask and become yourself." She is using her power to empower others.

I find great comfort in the guidance of others. I find myself reading, studying, and learning nonstop. This may not be your style. Going inward and getting direct answers may be what helps you the most. I do both. Choose what works for you. Honoring your style of learning and creating your own path is powerful and essential.

What do I have the power to do now?

What do I wish I had the power to do?

What is keeping me from having that power?

If I knew I could not fail what would I be doing now?

I choose, now, to develop the power to...

Reminder
COURAGE = feeling the fear and choosing to do something anyway
FEAR = **F**alse **E**vidence **A**ppearing **R**eal

Sources of Power = love, warmth, appreciation, gratitude, excitement, patience, commitment, vision, balance, courage, clarity, confidence, determination, flexibility, compassion…

Destroyers of Power = blame, shame, punishment, undermining, intimidation, domination, belittling, complaining, withholding, limiting beliefs, anger, rage, insensitivity, fear…

Understanding the Mind/Body/Spirit Connection

Choose not to seek approval. Have enough respect for yourself to know your own worth.

As said many times – our thoughts determine the choices we make and the actions we take – our behavior. In the past, the body and mind were treated as separate. We now *know* thoughts, feelings, and emotions produce chemicals in our bodies that can produce feelings, emotions, and thoughts. All of this can affect our physical, spiritual, and emotional health and wellbeing.

Candace Pert, in her book, *Molecules of Emotion*, described this process and explained how emotions, and the chemicals they produce, can support or inhibit body/mind processes.

Louise Hay spent a lifetime educating people on the practical aspects of the body/mind connection. In, *You Can Heal Your Life*, she listed illnesses and the emotions that lead to them.

Inna Segal in her book, *The Secret Language of the Body*, expands on and adds to this idea.

Masaru Emoto has studied the way thoughts, ideas, and words affect the structure of water molecules. He reminds us we are at least 75% water and asks us to consider how our thoughts and self-talk affect our wellbeing. Then to consider how our words affect others.

Try this just for fun. Take two small bowls of freshly cooked rice and cover them. Label one with loving supportive words and the other with hateful unsupportive words. Talk to them, whenever you walk past, in the same way. After a few days, notice what happens to the rice in each of the bowls. I did it and was shocked and amazed at the result.

The placebo effect is well known. In experiments, some people are given real medication and others are given sugar pills. They're both told that this is a powerful new drug that will help them. Often the people taking sugar pills have as much success as the people taking medication. The nocebo effect is just as powerful. When someone is told there is no medication that will help and they only have a short time to live, that is often what happens. It is the mind and the thoughts it is thinking that make the difference in what happens physically. Do we take time to settle our minds and listen to the voice within for guidance? Are we taking time to connect with the field that surrounds us? Do we pay attention to the metaphysical (thoughts and feelings) as well as the physical?

In what ways is my self-talk positive and supportive, or negative and toxic? What are some of the things I say to myself over and over? Are these things supportive, causing me to take action, or am I bullying myself?

Who are the toxic people in my life? What do they say? How do their words or actions make me feel and drain my energy? Is there a way I can bring this to their attention and request they treat me more considerately? I had a habit of letting things go until they built up over a long period of time and then I would explode with anger and resentment. Now, I choose to handle things with gentle strength, in a kind way, in the moment.

Who are the supportive people in my life? What do they say? How do their words or actions make me feel and encourage me? Have I told them how grateful I am for the way their words make me feel?

How are my words and actions supportive of others or toxic to them?

How do my feelings of self worth and care affect my choice of food (nutrient rich or empty calories)? How does this affect my energy level, mental attitude, and my power?

How do the choices I make to exercise or not exercise affect my thoughts and feelings about myself, as well as my wellbeing and power?

Are things going well or is it time to make changes? If needed, what are the changes I must make and when will I start?

Part Three

Nurturing and Nourishing My Earth Suit

When astronauts travel in space they must use a space suit. To be able to live on this planet we have been given an earth suit. It is strong, flexible, self-healing, adaptable, repairable, waterproof, and capable of amazing things. As we evolve, we consciously keep stretching what we once thought were the limits of the body/mind/spirit. Olympic winners do it constantly, as do scientists, explorers, and those of us who choose to test our own limits and grow.

We now know this earth suit is not just a body, or just a mind, but a complex arrangement of systems that all function together doing millions of things simultaneously, to keep us alive and functioning optimally on this planet, most often without any conscious effort on our part.

What we think, believe, focus on, and eat will all affect our wellbeing and that of those around us. *If we are to live the life we desire we must create health, resilience, and adaptability.* The habits we form over a lifetime support or challenge us. *Now* is always a good time to look at some recommended practices and see how ours measure up. Then, to tell ourselves, "Yes, well done!" or "Oops, time for some changes."

In this section we will focus on:

Self-Awareness
Life in Balance
The Power of Breath
Our Energy Systems
Movement and Exercise for Body/Mind/Spirit
Nourishment for Body/Mind/Spirit
Meditative Practices: Mindfulness, Yoga, Qigong…
Work and Play
Re-creation through Recreation
Becoming: Who Am I? Who am I Becoming?

PATH TO SERENITY

Have fun!!!

Think

Write

Draw

Be Silent

Laugh

Move

Explore and

Learn more about yourself!!!!

Self-Awareness

Those who get on in this world are those who, if they aren't happy with their circumstances, change.

How well do I know myself? How can I become more aware of my essence – my true self? Understanding who I am, and what has brought me to this place, is a beginning. Then *letting go* of old feelings, habits, and behaviors that no longer serve me allows me to *open* to new, unlimited possibilities.

A massive amount of information comes to us each day – much more than we can handle. Our perceptions have an automatic filtering system that limits what we see, hear, and feel. We must consciously focus our attention to sharpen our perceptions and perspective so we notice things we might otherwise miss.

How well do I know those close to me? What can I do to understand others better? It is said that we project on to others things we don't want to see or admit we do ourselves. Jesus said, "Why do you see the speck in your brother's eye, when you don't see the log in your own." Byron Katie in her book, *Loving What Is*, presents a method, which uses only four questions, to help people become more aware of their perceptions. She asks us to consider this: Things that bother us about others may actually be reflections of our own shortcomings.

Remember to listen carefully to yourself and to others. Often others are bringing us messages we need to hear. Ask, what is the bit of truth in what this person is saying to me? What is the bit of truth, or what is false, in the thoughts running through my mind?

Often, we discount our intuition and don't listen. Messages that come spontaneously can be extremely important. Often they provide insights, which if ignored can cause problems. We must learn to discern and then trust our intuition – our inner teacher.

People used to say, "I'll believe it when I see it." Wayne Dyer, a prolific self-awareness writer, said, "I'll see it when I believe it." Our beliefs can create limits and narrow our possibilities and opportunities, or they can lead us to new experiences and expanded awareness. We have the ability and the opportunity to create our own reality, and if we decide we don't like what we have created, to change it.

Writing is a tool that can help us learn what we know and don't know about ourselves and about the world. In her best selling book, *The Artist's Way*, Julia Cameron encourages her readers to do *Morning Pages*, by writing three journal pages every morning. When you are feeling good this writing will be creative and inspiring. When you are feeling down, this writing can provide a place to release frustrations, explore challenges, or reflect on personal issues. In the past, people have used this book as an inspiration to gather together with friends and work through it in a supportive group rather than totally on their own. It is effective either way.

I saw Kim Morrison interviewed recently. During the interview, she talked about the importance of self-awareness, self-acceptance, self-control, self-care, self-discipline, and self-respect. On my path, it was important for me to spend time in each one of these areas, evaluating where I was functioning and strengthening as needed. She has written a book called *The Art of Self Love*. Her vast knowledge, moving personal stories, and joy in sharing her wisdom made me feel her advice was well presented and critical.

In the *Wizard of Oz* the scarecrow was searching for a brain, the tin man for a heart, and the lion for courage. In the end they were each told that what they were searching for had been in them all along. That is the way it is. It's like the sun being covered by the clouds. It's always been there. We just need to wait for the clouds to clear, or to change the beliefs, habits, or feelings that keep us from having access to what is already at the core of our existence.

Use writing now to explore, answer questions, or *create your own questions*. Let your answers flow. Again, if you can't think of anything to write, just wait and *allow* the writing to come without planning. Listening to some gentle music may help. What comes may amaze you.

What are the core values of my true self? Our values drive all our decisions, often unconsciously.
If you need a list of values to help you think about this question, look on the Internet. There are many lists, as well as one created by Brené Brown from her book, Dare To Lead.

What do those around me value? How does that affect me?

What habits of behavior, positive or negative, do I notice in myself?

Which of my habits, thoughts, or behaviors benefit me and how?

Which would be best to release?

What can I do to alter my thinking or my behavior?

What do I want to create – or change in my life?

In what ways do I show self-acceptance and self-respect?

In what ways do I take care of myself?

How do I show self-control and self-discipline?

Now: *Set an intention that will help you to move toward one thing you wish to refine, change, or achieve. Write about it below. Breathe deeply. Let go, relax and trust. Act when it feels right.*

Trust: Trusting, and focusing positively on the result, is part of the "law of attraction" that so many are using today to create the life they desire. Who is going to create the life you desire if not you? Remember when you plant a seed you don't keep pulling it up to see if the root is growing – you *trust*.

Reminders:
1-When things are difficult, realize what is happening in the moment maybe essential for the eventual outcome, which can't be seen in the present. The folktale, *"Fortunately, Unfortunately,"* relates many situations in which an event appears unfortunate initially, but in the long run is truly fortunate. So often the extremely hard times we go through lead to amazing growth, change, and self-renewal.

2-We have choices, but in order to make them, our brain must be working effectively. In order to think clearly our brain must be well-nourished. When blood sugar levels drop and are too low, the frontal lobe, the thinking part of our brain, shuts down and thinking becomes unclear. Then the limbic system, the emotional part, takes over. We become frustrated, irritated, and have difficulty thinking clearly. Some people referred to this state as "hangry," hungry + angry. In order to handle life, and its many choices and decisions, we must be sure the body/mind is well fed. Remember, choices are best made when we are in the superpower of calm.

3-As you let go and replace old ways with new, staying calm and very focused is an important part of the process. I love the parable of the two wolves. *An old Cherokee brave was talking to his grandson about good and evil, when he explained there are two wolves battling inside each of us. One is evil. It is angry, jealous, greedy, resentful, and arrogant. The other is good and is joyful, peaceful, loving, and full of serenity and kindness. The grandson thought for a while and asked his grandfather, "Which one will win?" The grandfather answered, "The one you feed."* Yes, what we focus on, pay attention to, and feed in our lives, is what will flourish. We must be aware and careful where we place our attention and intention.

Life in Balance

When I married, I was a student. I quickly became a mother. Between completing a BA and MEd, and doing the best I could to be a caring compassionate mom, wife, and teacher, I lost all sense of life in balance.

In the 1980s I saw a cover of *Time* magazine that said, "*Stress is the Number One Cause of Illness.*" That was a radical concept at the time, but I took it to heart. Today, it is common knowledge. Lifestyle, not germs, is the main influencer of health. I got the feeling that in order to stay healthy, I needed to reduce stress and find more balance.

Then, my daughter, who was in college at the time, sent me a chart she created for me to use. It was so helpful that I have kept it over the years and have produced a version of it in this book.

My other daughter, who was living at home at the time, encouraged me to join her in an aerobics class. It reminded me of how essential movement is to our overall wellbeing. It also helped me remember I had been a dance major in college. A classmate had started a dance company that often performed in New York City, *Garth Fagan Dance*. They had a local evening community class in the town where I lived, which was their home base. I started attending this class. Eventually, I branched out and took classes in qigong and yoga. I was able to decrease stress and was on my way to a life in balance. By using movement, dance, yoga, qigong, and eating well, and working on creating balance in my life, I had started on the path to reduced stress and lifelong wellness. Keeping life in balance is a challenge *and* a reward. We must make sure we get enough:

- Nutrient dense food, vitamins, minerals, herbs, and time in the sun to absorb vitamin D
- Exercise: strength, endurance, balance, and flexibility
- Rest, relaxation, meditation, and listening
- Quality sleep
- Time for family and friends
- Personal time to think, dream, reflect, create, take hot baths, spend time attending to financial matters, create meaning and purpose in your life, walk in the rain, travel, pray, dance, meditate, read ...
- Meaningful work and service to others
- Spiritual time to connect with God, the universe, source, great mystery, your inner self, nature, all that is, your strength and power to....
- Recreation and play

In order to develop balance, we must first create awareness of where our time is spent. Fill in the charts on the following pages to show how much is spent in each area, each day. Then look to see where you are unbalanced and find ways to bring yourself back into balance. Do this every few weeks to update.

Here are three charts.

- One is an example.
- One is for you to fill in now.
- The third is for you to photocopy. Use it in the future, to help you learn what has fallen out of balance and needs readjustment.

PATH TO SERENITY

Fill in the full space if you did well, or half or one quarter or one eighth of the ideal amount.

☺	Monday	Tuesday	Wednesday	Thursday	Friday	Saturday	Sunday
Eat Well							
Exercise							
Sleep							
Personal Time							
Spiritual							
Friends and Family							
Rest/Relax Meditate							
Work							

♡	Monday	Tuesday	Wednesday	Thursday	Friday	Saturday	Sunday
Eat Well							
Exercise							
Sleep							
Personal Time							
Spiritual							
Friends and Family							
Rest/Relax Meditate							
Work							

PATH TO SERENITY

	Monday	Tuesday	Wednesday	Thursday	Friday	Saturday	Sunday
Eat Well							
Exercise							
Sleep							
Personal Time							
Spiritual							
Friends and Family							
Rest/Relax Meditate							
Work							

Based on the information gathered from these charts:

In what areas do I need to spend more time?

In what areas do I need to cut back a bit?

What else can I do to create more balance in my life?

The Power of Breath

Everything was ready. The group that had been here for a week had left. The houses were cleaned. The boat was on the way to town to pick up the new group. I was standing in the kitchen visiting with the staff. I heard a crash. A look out the window confirmed my worst fears. The water tower that served the kitchen, restaurant, main bathroom, yoga space, and five houses had just fallen over. It was lying on the ground in pieces.

The new group would arrive in a little over an hour. What could we do? I paused and took that very deep breath that always helps. The calm and serenity that flows quickly over me when something outrageous happens and causes a problem enveloped me. I paused a moment in silence, took another long deep breath, and listened.

My mind kicked into high gear. To the chef and his helper I said, "Please go to the small water tower at the Tongan house and drain it. Take it off the stand and bring it here with the fittings. Then go back and get the stand that it sits on." To the two who were raking, I said, "Please, go take the legs of the tower that has fallen and the broken tank and move them out of the way so we have a place to put the new water tower." Fortunately, the legs for one of our water towers were movable, so we didn't have to build a new one on the spot. The tank was up and filled with water before the group arrived. No worry, no fear, no spinning of wheels. Just calm, quick, *inspired* action.

I have a friend that reminds me of this every time I see her. She says, when she faces a difficult situation she thinks about what happened to me and in her mind says, "If Patti can handle a water tower falling over when guests are arriving in an hour, I can handle this situation."

Breath is a powerful tool. Many have not learned how to use it and do not understand why it is so effective. It can be used to create or change our state of mind, increase energy, move our nervous system from sympathetic (fight, flight, or freeze) to parasympathetic (rest, digest and create), or produce a meditative state. I learned about the power breath when I climbed a telephone pole at Miraval, a mindfulness focused spa in Arizona. When I stood on the top, the pole began to sway, reflecting my fear. It was with deep breathing I was able to get it to stop. Breath is a tool that has served me well.

Let's explore the power of conscious breathing. Take time to try the following breathing techniques. Then under each technique record how it made you feel and under what circumstances you might use it to change your feelings or state of mind.

Long, Slow, Equal In and Out, Deep Breathing

This is the breath I use most often in difficult situations, to take me quickly from a state of stress into a state of calm and serenity, from which I can handle and solve problems. It is the breath that most quickly takes us from sympathetic to parasympathetic when we are stressed.

It can also can calm and strengthen us and lead to a peaceful, meditative state.

Breathe, filling your belly first and then your lungs. If you wish, put your hands on your belly as you lie on your back to see if the breath really is coming into your belly first. Reverse as you exhale completely. Slow your breathing as much as possible by counting the seconds of the inhale and exhale. Is it possible to slow your breath to one or two breaths a minute or less? After you have a sense of how long your breath is, you can stop counting and just focus on the breath coming in and out, continuing to make it slower and slower.

When might you be able to use this breath?

Breath of Fire

It is said that the blood in your body passes through your lungs every three minutes. This breath will cleanse and oxygenate your blood and energize and calm your body/mind. Do an initial inhale and then focus on forcefully exhaling, over and over, through your nose. As you continue, the inhale will happen automatically so you can focus on the exhale. Keep your mouth closed and breathe in and out *only* through your nose so you don't hyperventilate. The goal is equal in and out breaths that can be done slowly or energetically for three minutes.

How did this make you feel?

Alternate Nostril Breathing

- Breathe through the left nostril only – the moon side – to relax and calm yourself or when falling asleep.
- Breathe through the right nostril only – the sun side – to energize yourself or when needing to wake up.
- Breathe through alternate nostrils – to create balance.

When doing alternate breathing use your finger or thumb to block the nostril through which you have just inhaled. Exhale through the nostril that is now open. Now inhale through the nostril through which you have just exhaled. Then close it with your thumb and exhale through the one that you just opened. Remember; always exhale through the nostril you have just opened.

Can you feel the difference?

Segmented Sniffs and Exhales

These can energize or calm the mind/body.
There're many different styles to use when doing this.

- 4 short sniffs in – 4 short sniffs out
- 8 shirt sniffs in – 1 long breath out through the mouth
- 8 short sniffs in – 8 short sniffs out
- One long breath in through the nose – hold for four counts – one long exhale out through the mouth
- Breath in through the nose for 5 counts – hold for 5 counts – breath out through the mouth for 5 counts – rest for 5 counts – repeat
- Experiment with these or more that *you create*. Record how they make you feel.

Which of these works best for you?

- During massage or exercise inhale deeply through the nose and exhale completely through the mouth to release tension, stress, hurt, pain, or anxiety.
- Breathing in and out only through your nose has been suggested as away of keeping you calm and relaxed throughout the day.

Breathing to Achieve Heart Brain Coherence

Achieving a coherent heart/brain state is taught at the Heart-Math Institute in California. It is a state from which we can effectively accomplish more. Put your hands in the area of your heart. Breathe slowly. Imagine breathing in and out through your heart. This will bring a feeling of relaxed safety. Then, as you breathe feel caring, compassion, love, or gratitude. This will help your heart move from a scattered irregular wave pattern into a coherent pattern of calm, regular waves. It is a powerful technique that I do many times a day to settle myself as I move forward, leading with my heart and embracing purpose and passion.

Heart/brain coherence is a powerful state which can be used to achieve important goals or to just "be." The Heart-Math Institute has many practices and tools to help achieve and monitor a coherent heart/brain state. Over the years they have accumulated extensive research that they share in books, articles, and monitoring devices. A visit to their website is worth the time and effort.

Could you feel the difference? How did it benefit you?

Our Energy Systems

There are many perspectives of how energy is produced or accessed and more are being discovered regularly. East Indians believe chakras are the energy centers of the body that must remain open and healthy in order to keep life force energy flowing. They believe this energy, which they call prana, can be regulated and all energy centers balanced, through the practice of yoga, conscious breathing, and meditation.

As I studied yoga, I acquired a basic understanding of the chakras. Each one is located in the area of a specific gland. When practicing yoga, these glands are stimulated by breathing, chanting, or slowly moving in and out of asana, the postures of yoga. Yoga has many gifts that will be discussed in another section but for now, think of the chakras as the part of the body practitioners of yoga believe create, balance, and maintain energy.

Another brief but more scientific explanation of energy in the body is that mitochondria, organelles that are actually ancient bacteria trapped inside each cell, produce ATP – adenosine triphosphate – a compound that fuels many processes in the living cells of the body. It is known as the primary energy carrier in all living organisms on earth.

Another concept is that we are solar powered beings. The light of the sun enters our body. It energizes us and helps us to produce vitamin D. Also, we eat plants that have been created by the interaction of sunlight with chlorophyll in the leaves as well as water and nutrients that come up from the earth. Therefore, when we eat a salad we are eating processed sunlight.

Have you noticed how your energy feels on a cloudy stormy day compared to how you feel on a bright sunny day? When it is cloudy and rainy we call that a low-pressure weather system. When it is bright and sunny we call it a high-pressure system. It is interesting how often our moods correspond. When the barometric pressure is low we often feel lazy or sad. When it is high we may feel energized and happy. Some people notice seasonal differences in energy due to changes in the amount and intensity of sunlight available.

The Chinese believe energy, which they refer to as Qi/Chi, flows through the body along lines called meridians. When Qi is blocked illness can occur. Acupuncture, acupressure, hand and foot reflexology, Qigong, and other energy medicine techniques are used to remove the blocks and allow the energy to flow freely again. This restores a state of balance and flow, thus health.

Toe Tapping: This is a simple way to build chi. Lie on your back, feet about eight inches apart. Tap your big toes together and then swing your feet apart so your little toes almost touch the surface on which you are lying. Think of the action of windshield wipers that go into the center and out to the sides of the windshield. Do this quickly and strongly for two to five minutes. Listening to music makes the time pass more quickly. This will increase the chi/energy in your body and can help improve a depressed state of mind. Rebounding or just bouncing in place has a similar effect and gets the lymph moving, which detoxifies and energizes your system.

The Japanese call this energy Ki and use Reiki or Shiatsu, a form of massage, to remove blocks.

There are many forms of hands-on energy healing: Reiki, Quantum Touch, Psych-K, EFT, Qigong, to name a few. It is our natural gift to help ourselves and others heal. Energy healing is a matter of intention as well as focused attention. It is based on praying or asking the life force energy to flow through us and on to another person to do the healing that is required. If you want to learn how to do this, read a book, take a class, or just focus your love through your hands, the way a mother does when she holds her sick child. *Essential Reiki* by Diane Stein is a great source. However, taking a weekend class with a Reiki master is best. Energy healing is gaining acceptance as we learn more about how it works and how we can access it. Once we feel this energy flowing through our hands, we totally understand.

Our energy comes from so many sources. Our attitudes and feelings can drain or increase our energy. Often, we feel more energized after a workout session or yoga class then we did before. Exercise can increase rather than drain our energy.

There are numerous perspectives on how we obtain energy and how we can use what we have gathered. Some come from scientists and some from healers. All are continuously expanding their understanding of energy. We are miraculous beings. Healing is moving from being thought of as a biological process, to being one that uses physics; light, sound, and vibration. It is from this perspective that energy healing is gaining acceptance. Feelings and emotion (energy in motion) respond well to energy healing.

Awareness of our body's energy systems is something we can cultivate. Our energy can affect our state of mind and those around us. We can send good energy/vibrations out to others or steal energy. Others can sap our energy or help it to increase.

What happens to your energy when an enthusiastic person supports or encourages you?

What happens to your energy when a controlling or demanding person reprimands, directs, or criticizes you?

Reflect on your interactions with others and notice if you are draining their energy or helping them gain energy.

Another Way of Viewing Chakra Energy

There is a theory that every seven years our life energy focus is in one of the chakras. Thus we are focused in the following areas *at the age indicated*. There is a flow, this is not exact, but a general guideline. Listed below are ages and the energy center focus during that time. A more complete explanation of this can be found in my first book, *Journey to Serenity*.

1-7   Root: Awareness of earth family, community, school, friends…
7-14   Sacral: Creativity
14-21   Solar Plexus: Power
21-28   Heart: Love
28-35   Throat: Self-expression
35-42   Third Eye: Vision
42-49   Crown: Spirituality

At age fifty, the process starts all over again at the base chakra, this time with more awareness.

49-56   Root: Re-evaluation of all aspects of our life, beliefs, social interaction, relationships, occupation, location of home, interests, health …
56-63   Sacral: Re-creating our present way of life or creating a new way of life
63-70   Solar Plexus: Power
70-77   Heart: Love
77-84   Throat: Self-expression
84-91   Third Eye: Vision for self and humanity
91-98   Crown: Spiritual connection

Use this page to write about the ways the information found on this chart matches what you have been experiencing in your life.

Movement and Exercise for Body/Mind/Spirit

Keeping physically active is the most important thing we can do to help us remain strong and flexible as we age and enthusiastically embrace change. It keeps us young and fit mentally, physically, and emotionally. There have been periods of my life when I have been so busy I have forgotten to exercise, dance, and sing, to my detriment.

In my mid-fifties I totally embraced dance, once again. It helped me overcome fear and gather courage. Dance is an amazing form of exercise. It allows freedom, creativity, flexibility, rhythm, balance, and all you need is your body and a bit of music. Then, for many years I got busy and forgot about its importance. Now, as I near eighty, I find that movement of all kinds is what keeps my muscles strong and my body from deteriorating and becoming frail. Even when we have let our physical wellbeing go for many years, focused attention and consistent effort makes regeneration an option. Currently, I dance and rebound in the ocean to build strength and help my lymph move and detox my system.

Movement has always been a passion of mine. I was a dance major in college but changed to teaching because dance did not fit into family life in those days. It is a joy to follow news of my classmate. His dance group, in their sixties, are still performing on stages around the world. When they were in their late thirties they thought their careers were about to end when they turned forty. They have used dance, movement, and yoga to keep themselves young, strong, and agile. Is my belief that they will keep performing professionally throughout their sixties and seventies. In the past, limiting beliefs stopped us. Now, continuing to use our bodies well helps keep us strong, flexible, and capable of more than we ever thought possible.

One thing I have learned in the last few years is the importance and value of good posture. In the past, when someone would mention it, I would think, that doesn't apply to me. But oh, was I wrong. It got to the point where my feet were pronated and I couldn't wear attractive shoes. Then my full posture prolapsed. As I walked my hands faced to the back and my shoulders and head tipped forward. Using the *Fixing You* books and videos by Rick Olderman, I began to learn more about posture and it's effect on deterioration of the body. I found that keeping my weight forward and directly over my feet, making sure my gluteus muscles were engaging as I walked, leading with my heart, and keeping my hands facing inward added strength to my legs and gluteus as well as more endurance and spring to my step. Over the last year I have taken off years of deterioration and aging. It is not that I feel and I need to stay young forever, but I feel it is essential to stay strong and resilient. I have learned not to let things go, thinking it is just aging. Most things are fixable with focus, intention, and attention. When fixed, they add strength and self-confidence to our lives. Yoni Whitten's, Pain Fix Protocol website is another excellent source.

Exercise is best done in a balanced way. Physical fitness is based on: Strength, Endurance, Flexibility, and Balance. There is a tendency to focus on one or two of these but not all four. As you focus on one of these areas physically, it is not only physical development that takes place but development of the mind, emotions, and attitude. Thus, when flexibility is improved physically, flexibility of thoughts, emotions, and attitudes also develops.

Exercise (exorcize) can affect our mental state and move us from depression to joy. Exercise produces endorphins, chemicals that change our mood for the better. Even ten minutes of vigorous body movement can change our mental state. If you feel you don't have time for full on exercise, just go outside and take a walk in the fresh air or put on some music and get up and shake your body or dance. It is important to get the muscles working and the lymph flowing to release toxins from your body that can build up from *too much sitting*. How much and what kind of exercise is a very personal matter.

From the list below choose some things you enjoy. The selection is ever expanding. Add more choices to the list. Circle those that interest you. Double circle those you chose to explore.

Run walk jump rope trampoline rollerblade windsurf kite surf surf swim ski hike climb bicycle dance tennis football rugby soccer volleyball Aikido Tai Chi Qigong yoga water ski snow ski snowboard basketball karate lifting weights golf paddle board kayak canoe rebound …

HIIT

High Intensity Interval Training has become a very popular way of exercising. There are many ways to achieve this, for example, one-minute of a high intensity exercise is done followed by a slow but active minute of recovery, and then another high intensity one-minute interval. This pattern can be kept up for ten to twenty minutes. The entire time gives you a quick, short, effective, session of exercise for those that do not have time for more. It is highly effective for losing weight, increasing your hormone levels, building muscle, and slowing the aging process. It is thought to be much better for your health than a long drawn out exercise session that can be exhausting and produce inflammation. You can find a variety of YouTube videos or smartphone Apps that will guide you through this process.

Guidelines

- Exercise must be fun and rewarding or you won't do it. Choose something you enjoy.

- Exercise must include strength, endurance, flexibility, and balance if you wish to be physically fit and healthy.

- Spinal flexibility helps keep you young, strong, and fit. Flexibility of the spine and good balance are used as a measure of physical age. Your physical age can be older or younger than your chronological age depending on your lifestyle.

- If possible, schedule your exercise first thing in the day. It is energizing and calming and you will work more efficiently and effectively all day long. It is worth getting up a bit earlier to take care of yourself first. This helps you value and respect yourself. Remember the instructions you hear every time you travel by plane, "Put on your own oxygen mask first and then help those around you." Starting your day by taking care of yourself first is a powerful practice. If it is not possible to fit it in first thing in the morning, then be sure you fit something in during your day or evening.

- Breathe consciously as you exercise. Inhale on the preparation and then always exhale on the exertion of each movement. Focus on breathing with the movements as you exercise.

PATTI ERNST

Use this page to write about your experiences with exercise, what you enjoy most, and what you plan to do to expand your interests...

Nourishment for Body/Mind/Spirit

Becoming educated about food has become quite complex. By educating yourself, and sorting out what works for you, you can make it simple. Many outstanding books cover this subject in great detail. There are numerous websites, online summits, and groups with recommendations, as well as online coaches and classes. John and Ocean Robins are passionate advocates for healthy eating and their website might be a good place to start. Books by Mark Hyman MD are another great source for up to date information.

Some people say high fat and some say low fat, but they all say there are good fats and bad fats, so it is important to stick to those that will support health and avoid those that cause problems. Plant fats, such as avocados, nuts, olive oil, avocado oil, and coconut oil are considered excellent sources of fat. Trans fats and deep fried foods are problematic.

Diet is something that is person-specific and it is hard to generalize. It is up to you, with the help of personal research or a health care professional, to decide what is best for your body, age, and the amount you exercise. One thing for sure is that the standard American diet, SAD, is no longer keeping us healthy and we need to find a new approach. If we wish to grow healthy and have the energy to do what we desire, it is our personal responsibility to educate ourselves and change as we learn.

The following is a brief summary of some of what is known today about eating meals that energize, inspire, and support us mentally, emotionally, and physically. Remember: Optimal brain function is dependent on a well-nourished body. Your ability to think and make good choices can be affected by what you eat. Empty, or too few calories, can affect brain function adversely.

Nourishment takes many forms. We nourish mind and spirit by reading good books, spending time with friends, helping others, using our imagination, taking a hot bath, getting a massage, working through and resolving emotional issues, or using our five senses to experience life consciously. Processing and digesting our emotions is a type of nourishment that is rarely discussed but unprocessed, undigested, emotions can lead to many problems, among them the improper digesting of food.

Guidelines for Eating Consciously

- It is only in recent years that awareness and understanding of the gut micro biome has come to our attention. The gut is the home of millions of helpful as well as detrimental bacteria that affect every aspect of our lives. This is where a major part of our immune system is found. The gut is connected to the heart and brain via the Vagus nerve, the longest nerve in the body, which carries nine times as many messages to the brain as away from the brain. It is essential to gain an understanding of how the food we eat, and the emotions we feel, affect balance in the micro biome and stimulate the Vagus nerve. This nerve also has a major effect on our facial expressions, tone of voice, self-confidence, and over all sense of well-being.

- Prepare meals that are colorful and pleasing to the eye. Eat mindfully and pay attention to colors, flavors, and textures. Colorful foods tend to be nutrient dense and vitamin rich. Each color is produced by specific phytonutrient that is essential for good health.

- Eat mainly whole, unrefined, complex carbohydrates in the form of vegetables as well as some carefully selected whole grains, proteins, and fats.

- Avoid processed foods as they contain large amounts of sugar and unhealthy fats. They can leave your body under-nourished and prone to disease.

- Keep alcohol and sugar to a minimum. Artificial sweeteners also have adverse affects on the body. Honey and maple syrup are good natural sweeteners.

- A small amount of red wine and dark chocolate are said to be acceptable as a good source of antioxidants. This is debatable; so listen to your body and your feelings to see what they tell you about what is right for you.

- Some people do well with two meals a day. Others need three. Some do best with six small snacks a day. Your body will let you know. Listen.

- Food can be used as medicine when we carefully choose what to include or exclude. Nutritional healing is becoming more valued, in many cases, than taking medication. Many diseases can be cured or improved by our food or supplement choices. Often people are switching, when possible, from the Pharmacy to the Farmacy.

- Bananas and milk can help you fall asleep. Chocolate boosts the neurotransmitter serotonin and helps you feel happy.

- The percentage of each of the following changes continually. Be sure you include them all, but the portions are up to your body and the information you have acquired.
  - Complex Carbohydrates - vegetables, fruits, grains ...
  - Protein - tofu, cheese, fish, chicken, grass fed beef, eggs, beans and rice...
  - Fat - olive oil, nuts, olives, avocado, coconut oil, avocado oil...

- Ayervedic health practices suggest that including six tastes in all meals we eat helps us feel full and remain satisfied longer. The six tastes include salty, sweet, pungent, sour, astringent and bitter. To get details on which foods supply these tastes look on the Internet or in a book on Ayerveda. Adding herbs and spices adds more tastes.

- Remember, as in many areas of life, "Less is more." Focus on eating slowly and consuming smaller portions and be careful not to over eat.

- Recent findings have helped scientists and doctors to understand that inflammation is one of the main causes of most diseases. An anti-inflammatory diet is made up of all natural, unprocessed foods. This can keep you healthy and help you age slowly. Turmeric is an outstanding anti-inflammatory spice.

- In the book *Super Foods*, by Pratt and Matthews, there is a list of foods that support an anti-inflammatory diet.

Apples, avocados, beans, blueberries, broccoli, cinnamon, dark chocolate, dried fruit, olive oil, garlic, honey, yogurt, kiwi fruit, oats, onions, oranges, pomegranate, pumpkin, soy, spinach, tea, tomatoes, turkey, wild salmon, and walnuts are recommended in this book. It has been a long time since this book was published so some of these may have changed, but it is remarkable how most of them are still valid. This list can be expanded to include more varieties of a certain food. For example, blueberries may be best, but all types of berries are excellent.

- Being on an island overgrown with coconuts, we have paid special attention to the benefits of eating coconut in the form of oil, cream, milk, grated, flour … The amazing health benefits of coconut can be found online as well as in the book, *The Everything Coconut Diet Cookbook* by Sandage and Bull, which also has extensive excellent recipes.

- Today, many are concerned about the use of wheat flour. Use alternative flours made from almonds, coconut, chickpeas, quinoa, rice …

- *Playing With Your Food.* When I was in Hawaii I always wanted to write a book with that title. There were so many foods I used for different purposes than to eat. Here are just a few. Papaya skins are wonderful to rub on the skin to soften it and slow wrinkles. Eating papaya seed is anti-parasitic. I loved to go to the beach, take an avocado, mix it with soft sand, and rub it all over my body and hair. I'd let it dry and then go for a swim. It is a scrub that leaves my skin exfoliated and moisturized. Avocado oil mixed with sea salt and lemon juice, in equal parts, can be rubbed into the scalp to clean and revitalize.

Oatmeal can be used to do a facemask. When you make hummus, save a bit to do an exfoliating, moisturizing, mask. Fresh lemon or lime is an excellent deodorant. This is just a start. Create some of your own.

- Be sure to eat organic whenever possible. The Environmental Working Group, EWG.org. publishes much information to help you in this area.

- Herbs, spices, and some mushrooms are important for good health. There are so many they must be looked up on the Internet. I have a book that lists the ones used in the practice of Ayerveda, East Indian medicine. Herbs can be used in the process of cooking, as tea, or taken in supplement form. Turmeric when used with a bit of black pepper is one of the best anti-inflammatory spices known. It and many other herbs, can be mixed into eggs, soups and even smoothies. It can also be used topically on cuts and scrapes to help them heal faster. Ashwaganda and Rhodiola are adaptagenic herbs that help us modulate the effects of stress. Ginkgo helps increase blood flow to the brain and sharpens thinking and memory. The list of herbs and spices with exceptional benefits goes on and on. These are powerful plants that have been used for healing since ancient times.

- Food Preparation: This helped me in the years when I was working full-time and had a family. I continue to do this to this day. When vegetables are brought home I immediately wash and dry them with a salad spinner. Food fits better into the refrigerator, lasts longer, and when it comes time to cook or make a salad most of the preparation work is done and the final mixing is quick and easy. This way you can eat healthy nutrient-rich "fast food" in less time than it takes to go out for a meal of nutrient-poor fast food. Create your own recipes that are quick, easy, and nutritious.

- Eating Out: This can be saved for special occasions. When you do eat out you can relax and enjoy it, or if you are health-conscious, choose simple raw or lightly processed food following these guidelines above.

- Sugar: Read, *Sugar Blues,* by William Dufty or *Lick the Sugar Habit*, by Nancy Appleton. Then decide what to do about this hazardous food. They are older books but are still powerful and available online.

- Snacks: Prepare vegetables and dip them in plain yogurt or oil with some Italian seasoning added. Fresh or dried fruit, nuts, sunflower seeds, or pumpkin seeds are easy. Apples and cheese or celery and tree nut butters are healthy and quick to prepare.

Use these guidelines and be creative. Look up recipes online that use alternative ingredients you know are healthy. Design some daily meal plans and recipes for yourself. Remember to keep them easy and nutritious.

PATTI ERNST

Snacks to Nourish My Earth Suit

PATH TO SERENITY

Meals to Nourish My Earth Suit

Meditative Practices

There are many meditative practices. Most are used to quiet the mind. We might relax in silence or listen to a guided meditation and allow inspiration to flow. The "monkey mind" dashes around thinking outlandish thoughts and having erroneous imaginings. Meditation helps focus the mind. It helps us observe our thought process and understand how our mind works so we can focus on making changes. It helps one gain control rather than being controlled by emotional hijackings or obsessive thinking.

Meditation can be an end in itself; time to stop and settle the mind. Time to come to a place of complete stillness in a busy world. I am reminded of the movie, *The Last Samurai*, in which it is often said of a person, "too many minds," meaning the person is trying to act while still thinking. He has not settled his mind first so the action can take place without thought, making it faster and more precise. I learned how this works when I ran on the hard, irregular, crusty lava in Hawaii described in *Journey to Serenity*.

Meditation changes the way we deal with events and life situations. A regular meditation practice will build our ability to respond rather than react unconsciously. We develop greater self-awareness and have a better sense of peace, openness, and caring for our environment and those in it. Meditation can take us to a place we have never been before or to a place of stillness that allows us to hear the still small voice within. It is said prayer is when we talk to God and meditation is when we listen.

The Relaxation Response

This easy form of meditation for beginners developed by Herb Benson at Harvard is used to relax and calm the mind. In the early sixties he was able to make the use of meditation acceptable to mainstream society and medical practice.

The process: Breathe slowly and deeply. Repeat the same word (mantra) on each exhale. Choose any word that has a peaceful relaxing meaning for you. Herb suggests using the word ONE. Start with one to five minutes in the morning and in the evening, and increase, as you feel comfortable.

Does this help you feel more relaxed and at peace?

Progressive Relaxation

Lie down and close your eyes. Focus on one part of the body at a time. Tense it tightly as you inhale. Then release and relax it as you exhale. Move from foot to head until the entire body is relaxed.

How did this make you feel?

Guided Healing Meditation

Guided Imagery for Self Healing by Dr. Martin L Rossman teaches the use of guided meditation for insight into illness and healing. He has recorded a series of audios to support the use of the meditations.

One process: Relax, breathe deeply, and focus on your symptom. Then create a mental picture of it (rake, star, wooden block, tangled wire – what ever it feels like to you). Then ask your image/symptom what message it has for you. Often an illness or symptom is the body's way of trying to get our attention so we can focus on an issue and heal. It may seem silly, but asking and listening to what our body needs, can give amazing insights and lead to healing. Years ago, this process helped me get in touch with my symptoms and release emotional issues that were causing problems. The work of Dr. Rossman brings awareness to the power of the body/mind connection and the use of it to support the healing process.

What did you learn from your symptom?

Prayer

Prayer can be a meditative practice. Sometimes prayer takes the form of giving thanks. Sometimes prayer is a request. It is said that if we pray and ask for something, we then need to feel like it has already been given. We need to *trust* that when we ask, our prayers will be answered and have the faith to continue on as though it has already been received. That way you remain in a place of gratitude rather than a place of need.

Sometimes we pray in a very quiet place. Sometimes it is done with a journal in hand asking questions and listening for answers. Sometimes it is done in the form of a song. At other times when just being in nature or arranging flowers, prayers of gratitude pour fourth. Often, being in the present moment and focused can be a prayer. Write in a journal about your experiences with prayer.

Mindfulness

In *The Power of Now*, Eckhart Tolle wrote about the power of truly living in the present moment – not in the memories of the past or the fears or dreams of the future. Deepak Chopra said, "The past is the dream, the future is imagination, but the present is the gift, and that is why it is called the present."

Mindfulness is a practice that comes from the Buddhist tradition. It involves being present in the moment, remaining awake and aware, living consciously, and making responsible choices, not just reacting. Jon Kabat-Zinn wrote *Full Catastrophe*

Living, about his use of mindfulness in a hospital setting and how it brought about profound calmness and clarity of mind for hundreds of people. Today, the medical community has accepted mindfulness as a tool for helping heal stress-caused illnesses.

The practice of mindfulness helps us observe our surroundings, our thoughts, our breath, and keeps our focus in the present moment and calm. It helps us to stay out of past and future thinking. The only power we have is in the present moment. So often in today's world we take on enormous amounts of anxiety by reliving the past over and over or imagining too many future possibilities.

Mindfulness Reminders:

1- When in a stressful situation or feeling overwhelmed, take a moment to step back and look at the larger picture rather than remaining caught in the intensity of the moment. Pause, breathe, and look again with new eyes. When stress is overwhelming and intense, look around and slowly name the objects in your environment. This is a tool to help focus intensely in the moment in order to eliminate fear or anxiety.

2- Develop an awareness of your attitudes and feelings in different situations. Are you feeling positive, determined to keep going, inspired, ready to let go and trust, joyful, and grateful or are you feeling depressed, sad, overwhelmed, or ready to give up? Then consciously celebrate your feelings, or change them, depending on what will serve you best. Sometimes I find myself suddenly saying, *I don't need to be feeling this way. I stop in that moment, take a deep breath and make another choice about the way I am feeling.* It is amazing when we discover we have that sort of power and control over our emotions.

3- Change your perspective and look again. Become the *observer* of the situation rather than remaining enmeshed it.

4- Slow down and become aware. Smell the flowers, walk slowly noticing small things. Really look at the clouds, the sparkle of sunlight on the water, the plant growing out of the crack in the sidewalk, or truly notice the taste of an apple.

5- Meditate: Quiet the mind from all the chatter that tends to fill it. Create stillness for yourself.

6- Breathe: Ten slow, mindful, deep, equal inhales and exhales can change your state of mind.

7- Be curious. Enjoy living in the *Mystery* instead of in the *Know*. Ask questions instead of thinking you know the answers. It is said, the quality of our questions determines the quality of our lives.

8- Relax and focus. Take time to stretch your body. Resist the urge to multitask. Rather, stay focused intently on one thing at a time.

9- Become aware of the quality of your self-talk.

10- Take the time to talk with others on a deep level, about things that really matter. Speak your truth and really listen to the true insights and feelings of others. Intimacy (in to me see) is essential for mindful communication.

11- Ask yourself, am I using my own resources (time, energy, money, knowledge, wisdom) and those of the planet wisely, in a way that is helpful, not detrimental to self and others? Am I leading a sustainable existence? Too much food causes overweight bodies. Too many possessions possess us. Too much consumerism causes clutter in the dwelling and in the mind.

Develop an Attitude of Gratitude

The more we appreciate what we have, the more we receive. Many suggest keeping a gratitude journal beside your bed to use every morning or evening. Even just lying in bed and mentally going over the good things that have happened during the day is enough. When you awaken in the morning, giving thanks that you're still alive and reviewing the joy you expect to happen during the day is better than immediately focusing on problems or your to-do list. Begin the day by consciously choosing a great attitude, gratitude.

Take time to fill in the petals of this flower with things for which you are grateful.

Qigong

There are many systems for the conscious gathering of energy and the focused use of that energy. Qigong, and Tai Chi, a type of qigong, use energy in specific ways to protect and nurture one's self, or help others heal.

Qigong is used extensively in China. It is a practice of meditative movements used to gather or disperse Qi and keep it moving smoothly. Chinese believe Qi moves in meridians that run throughout the body and that a block in any meridian is what causes illness. Qigong practice helps one gain strength, balance, excellent posture, energy flow, and wellbeing. I studied this for the three years I spent in Alaska and felt it made a huge difference in my ability to handle life situations and stay healthy. It can be used for personal healing but can also be used by a trained practitioner who collects Qi and projects it when treating others.

The goal of Chinese medicine is to keep people healthy rather than allow sickness to get a foothold and create the need for intervention by a doctor. I feel the potential for the use of medical Qigong for energy healing will be explored worldwide in years to come. The book, *The Web That Has No Weaver*, by Ted Kaptchuk is an excellent source of information about Chinese medicine. It helps us become aware of the vast difference between medical practices in China and the Western world.

The Way of Qigong, by Kenneth S. Cohen is a comprehensive book on the healing qualities and the history of Qigong. Qi is life energy that must move easily and not become blocked or stagnant. Gong means work. Thus Qigong is working with life energy. We are part of nature and share Qi with all around us. Learning to control the flow and distribution of Qi improves the health of body and mind. Self-healing exercise, meditation, breathing, and self-massage practices are done daily for at least twenty minutes.

Qigong resembles a slow dance and is appropriate for all ages. As we move externally the mind remains calm, peaceful, and at rest. Qigong is empowering and fosters self-reliance and responsibility. It helps improve health and prevent disease. Stress, worry, and poor health habits disburse Qi. Qigong helps us gather and direct Qi. There are many of different styles of Qigong, but the basis of all is balance, relaxation, breathing, and posture. The goal is fully flowing Qi.

Yoga

Yoga is a powerful meditative, spiritual, and transformative practice that focuses on awareness, guidance, flexibility, strength, balance, and endurance for body, mind, and spirit. There are many different styles of yoga. Take classes in a few different types to learn which is most appealing to you.

Yoga means union. It is a conscious practice of breathing, movement, mantra, and asana designed to connect the finite essence of ourselves with the all-powerful infinite. It can clear and calm the mind, strengthen and energize the body, and create confident wellbeing. Yoga raises the energy of the body and calms the mind at the same time. A daily morning yoga practice can change your state of mind, the flow of your day, and the amount of energy you have available.

Yoga comes from the Hindu tradition. It is a practice I have engaged in since my twenties. In my fifties my focus turned to Kundalini, the yoga of awareness. I did my teacher training in Canada. I then began a practice called Sadahna every morning for two hours between five am and seven am, after which I got ready and left for my hour-long drive through the countryside to work on the edge of town. *Kundalini Yoga Guidelines for Sadahna – Daily Practice*, a book by my teacher Guru Charan Singh, helped me design a practice to fit my needs. It enabled me to grow, overcome fear, gain strength, energy, courage, and confidence. I became a very different person by caring for myself first, each morning, and then facing my day with greater amounts of patience and gentle strength.

It is said that if you do yoga for many years your physical age will be twelve years younger than your chronological age. I was not doing yoga for that reason, however, today at seventy-nine, I certainly feel more like I'm in my sixties, not almost eighty.

I tell my yoga classes that chronological age is determined by the number of times the Earth has gone around the sun since we were born. Our physical age is measured by how strong we are, how well we can balance, the flexibility of our spine, and how we feel. It is also measured by our enthusiasm, energy level, resilience, vitality, and emotional strength.

Similar to Qigong, Yoga focuses on life energy, which in Hindu it is called Prana. The goal is keeping the energy centers, called chakras, clear and open. Each center is in the area of a gland or glands that are stimulated as we move in and out of asana. Asana are considered static poses, in some styles of yoga. In Kundalini, asana are processes of movement into and out of a pose that stimulate and affect change in a gland, muscle, chakra, nerve plexus, attitude, or state of mind.

My experience over the years is that daily yoga, even if it is a short sun salutation as seen in the book *The Seven Spiritual Laws of Yoga* by Deepak Chopra and David Simon, is a beautiful technique for stress release and connecting with our essential self. Stress can create an environment in which disease can gain a foothold, therefore releasing stress is an essential practice. The book I use currently to guide my daily practice is, *The Kundalini Yoga Experience*, by Guru Dharam S. Khalsa and Darryl O'Keeffe.

The Eight Limbs of Yoga

There are eight limbs of yoga. These are often overlooked in yoga classes. I list them here, briefly, to create a picture of the richness available in a complete yoga practice.

1. *Yamas* – Self Control: do no harm, compassion, truth, use of vital energy, non-grasping, gratitude
2. *Nyamas* – Observance of Duty: inner and outer cleanliness, content with what we have

3. *Asana* – Posture: physical practice
4. *Pranayama* – Breath Control: breathing practice
5. *Pratyahara* – Withdrawal of the Senses: release sense perceptions, let go of distraction
6. *Dharana* – Concentration: shift of awareness
7. *Dhayana* – Meditation: focus
8. *Samadhi* – Absorption in the Divine: deep peace, no time, silence

Journal Writing

A journal is a fantastic place to write down your thoughts and feelings or to ask questions.

Get into a meditative state, ask questions, expect the answers to come, and listen carefully.

This is a powerful practice, which can often bring clear answers that you can act on immediately.

Remember to **ASK. A**sk and you shall receive. **S**eek and you shall find. **K**nock and the door shall be opened.

Experiment and Experience

Plan a time to reach out, explore, and get involved in some of these self-care/meditative practices. Commitment to one or more of these areas will be life-changing. Take time to enjoy a few. List those that appeal to you most.

Think and write about your experiences with meditative practices.

Which feel right for further exploration or commitment?

Work/Play/Sleep

*"We don't stop playing because we grow old.
We grow old because we stop playing."*
George Bernard Shaw

Work must be rewarding and something you truly enjoy. It has been said, "Choose work you love and you will never work another day in your life." It will seem like play. Work, well chosen, is a form of worship, according to Bahaullah, the founder of the Baha'i faith. Kahlil Gibran in *The Prophet* said, "Work is love made visible."

Our attitude toward the work we do is critical. We can create a job we love, or we can chose to love and appreciate the job we have. Many people are doing simple jobs, which allow them to serve. Cleaning an office after the people have left for the day is serving the people who will arrive the next morning. Driving a bus, delivering mail, waiting tables, or cooking school lunches can all be meaningful jobs. It is just how we feel about them, our perspective, and how much love we can put into them. To paraphrase Mother Teresa, life is not about doing something great, but doing something small with great love.

If our work is not something we care about deeply, it might be worth considering a change. When we think of the number of hours we spend each day involved in work, it is essential that we are doing something that is meaningful, brings joy, and fulfills our purpose. If not, it could make our life stagnant or uncomfortable. Often a change of job can take a while and needs to be accomplished slowly, mindfully, and carefully so as not to make things worse. Sometimes it requires the courage to move consciously and quickly. Either way we must practice discernment.

As time goes on, if work is to be enjoyable and have meaning and satisfaction we must find our purpose and passion. Then, we can move in that direction, find what we can do to be of service, and contribute to the well-being of humankind. In retirement, we can remain productive by looking deeply, finding the things that need to be done, and contributing our time, energy, wisdom, and resources to a situation or cause that moves us deeply and will make a significant difference. Remember Winston Churchill said. "We make a living by what we get. We make a life by what we give."

How do I feel about the work I do?

What changes, if any, do I need to make?

What am I passionate about? What do I love doing? What am I good at? How can I use my passion and skills to create meaningful work and be of service?

Children use play to practice what they will be doing when they grow up. Can we use play in the same way? It is worthy of some thought. I used challenging play when I was trying to overcome fear and gather enough strength and courage to leave a situation I needed to change.

What is play for you? For some it is participation in sports. For some it is watching sports. For some it is hiking, dancing, singing, or camping. For others it is golf and tennis. Many enjoy playing cards, contemplation, or getting lost in a great movie or meaningful book.

Play has so many possibilities. It is something we need to think about and enjoy. For me playing the guitar, dancing, hiking, yoga, snorkeling, and reading are things that bring me joy. I enjoy individual sports. Others love team sports. I enjoy participating, not watching others have all the fun. There are those who enjoy sitting, relaxing, and watching.

How often do I take time to play?

What are the things that feel like play to me?

Remember
Play takes many forms. What one person sees as play another may see as misery.

Play can be productive but it must be uplifting and joyful. It can exercise the mind or the body. It can allow us to totally let go and relax. Be sure to schedule some fun each day. If you don't schedule it, the urgencies of life will take over and wipe out all the playtime.

**Always remember the healing power
of laughter and hugs.**

Sleep, high quality sleep, is essential for good health. For years people thought sleep was optional. In preparing for a test students would stay up all night studying. Doctors, during your residency, would work days on end without any sleep. Today we realize sleep is critical. We must get enough uninterrupted sleep if we are to function optimally. While we sleep, the brain cleanses itself and performs many functions that prepare us for the next day.

Re-Creation through Recreation

This thought, *re-creation through recreation*, came to me when I lived in Hawaii. Looking back that is what I did when I chose to change my life and reinvent myself. I traveled, read, sang, played guitar, roller bladed, wind surfed, sailed, danced, explored, sat in silence, and sat in awe.

We need to do what we are meant to do and what our heart leads us to. We must move toward what we love and what brings us pleasure and joy. We must stop judging ourselves and others. One of my favorite songs by Steve Suskin says," We've got to save a little judgment, for judgment day!"

Recreation is another word for play. It is often through play that humans practice what they want to accomplish in their lives. When I needed to overcome fear, I learned to rollerblade, ice climb, windsurf, rock climb, and participated in many other challenging activities – playful activities which I needed to help me overcome fear on a physical level so I could move forward fearlessly on an emotional level. Facing challenges, developing new habits, and embracing new forms of play helps us to grow.

Is it time to make some big changes or is it time to make some tiny little adjustments? If so inspired, use some recreation time to re-create your life. Pursue some challenging activities. Step outside of your comfort zone and do something totally new. Let go of that which no longer serves you. Jewel sings, "No longer lend your strength to that which you wish to be free from. Live your life with love and bravery, and you shall lead the life uncommon." Remember, courage comes from and is produced by the heart. Start leading with your heart.

Write about your feelings as you are <u>planning</u> to step outside of your comfort zone. It can be scary. Release your feelings on these pages.

How do I feel when I think about doing _____?

What is the worst thing that could happen?

PATTI ERNST

What is the best thing that could happen?

Have a conversation with, or write a letter to your self.

Have a conversation with, or write a letter to source/God.

Write a letter to you from your ninety-year-old self.

Write about your feelings <u>after</u> you have tried something new, taken some risks or made some changes. How did it feel? What were you able to accomplish?

Playful goal setting:
Write down what you want to accomplish during the next year. Then put it away and don't look at it for a year. Enjoy life and play. Open it after one year and you will be amazed at how many things on that list have now been accomplished.

PATH TO SERENITY

Write a letter from universe to you.

Write a letter from you to the universe.

Becoming!
Who Am I Now?
Who Am I Becoming?

Becoming! Becoming takes time. It is about taking care of yourself, healing old wounds, forgiving yourself and others. It is about being curious and open to possibilities. It is about taking risks, letting go, being resilient, finding your gifts and talents, and deciding how best to use them. It is about journeying through hard times and dark nights of the soul with an attitude of gratitude because you know you will make it through and emerge stronger. It is about having strength, courage, and faith. Remember, "We are the ones we have been waiting for."

You can take this journey at any age. You will embrace it when you are ready. If you do it when you're younger it will enrich the way you live your life for a longer time. If the opportunity to make changes comes in mid-life, as it did for me, starting in my fifties, there is still a world of possibilities and opportunities that await you. It can be a whole new lifetime of overcoming fear, embracing experiences, and working toward becoming a conscious elder who can influence others.

If you choose a later time in life, as I am doing *once again* as I start my 80th trip around the sun, you still have many years until you reach ninety-five, which is when those in Okinawa believe you become a wise old elder – the community leader. There is always time to walk this path and take this journey. Becoming is what this life is about, and even when we release our earth suit and move on, we are still becoming. Here are seven possible steps you might take as you travel this path.

1. **Remembering** what you love, your current interests, your dreams, your desires and *discovering* what you feel needs to change in your life and in the world.
2. **Evaluating** your body/mind/spirit from a place of love and creativity while choosing the physical, emotional, and meditative practices which will support you on your journey. For example, I spent a year releasing fifty pounds of extra weight, which allowed me to move with more energy and resilience.
3. **Releasing** is a powerful process of letting go of old thoughts, ideas, hurts, perspectives, beliefs, and habits.
4. **Creating** new habits. Loving yourself enough to get ample sleep, eating well, moving or exercising often, incorporating new meditative or spiritual practices that will support you as you change and allow you to live fearlessly while having fun on the way. Getting beyond your comfort zone and trying new things.
5. **Awakening** and becoming aware of who you are and what needs to be done in your life and in the world. You might hear a call to the hero's journey. Be prepared to go through many dark nights of the soul and know they are all part of the process. Going through hard times helps you to change and become your new stronger self. Then bravely speaking up and allowing your voice to be heard.
6. **Embracing** patience. Having fun, taking care of yourself, and helping others along the way allows your life to flow and you to grow. Take plenty of time making the right decisions. Do not hesitate to review, revise, reevaluate,

and restate your goals. No one but you is rushing you to become, before you are ready.
7. **Deciding** gradually where you will put your passion, power, and energy – what you will eventually do. Once the decision has been made, create a sacred time and space for yourself in which you can light some candles, listen to some beautiful music, and draw a picture of your future. Imagine where you are, what you are doing, and especially how you feel. Create this with deep knowing, emotion, excitement, focus, and passion. When finished put it away in a safe place and allow the universe to work its magic.

Hopefully, by playing in this book you have become more aware and awake. Maybe you are feeling more joyful and satisfied with what you are currently doing or maybe you have made plans to make some changes. They may be very subtle and small, or they may be major. You may progress step-by-step over a long period of time, or take a sudden leap of faith. This section is a place for you to summarize, after you have finished the book, where you were, where you are now, and where you are going.

Our lives are filled with opportunities. There are many ways to learn and grow. Some are active and require doing. Some require quiet being.

Remember we are human beings not human doings.

PATH TO SERENITY

Who am I?

My Personality - How do others see me?

My Essence - My inner or true self.

My Essence Expressed Through my Personality - How I Want Others to See Me.

PATH TO SERENITY

PATTI ERNST

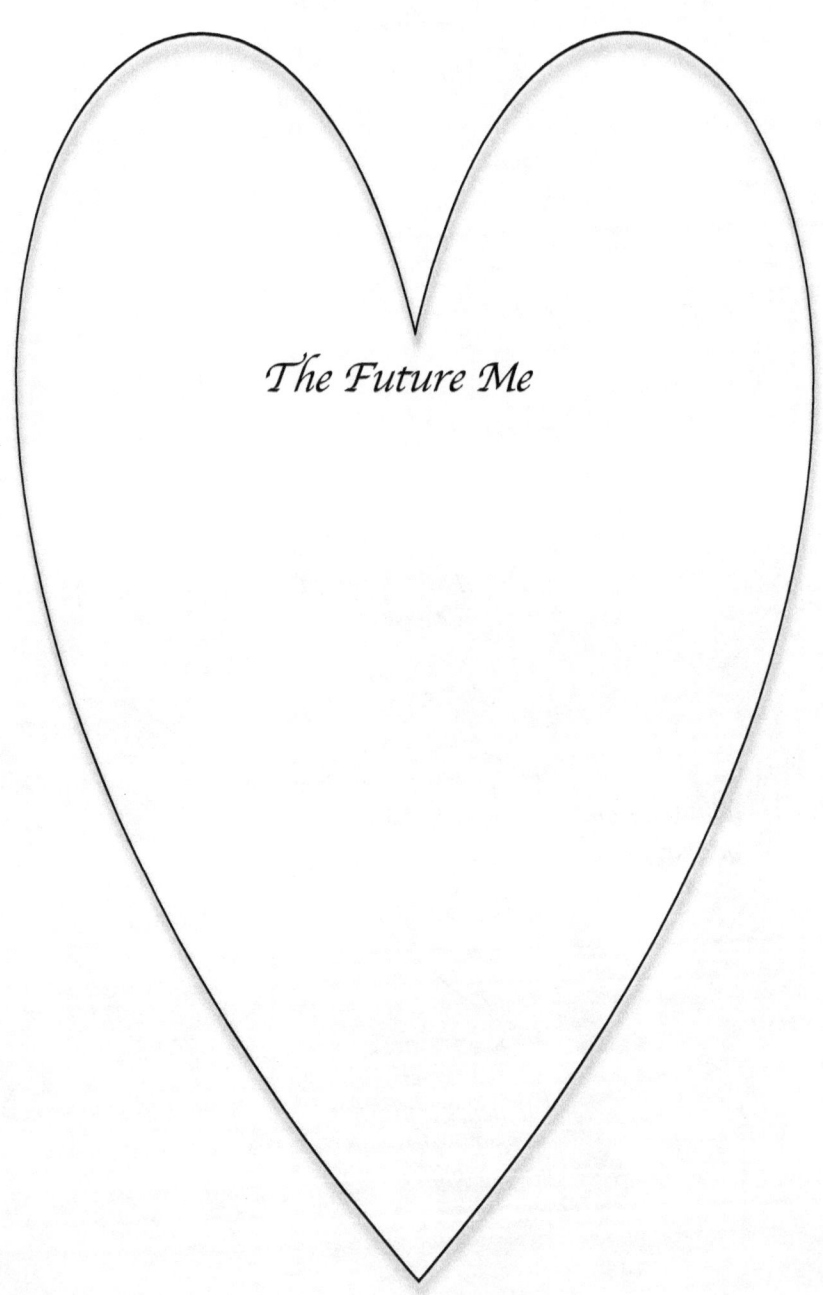

The Future Me

Epilogue

Sometimes people are living the life of their dreams. They are living in integrity, joy and fulfillment. For many people, there comes a time when they realize they are not living the life they are meant to be living. They have the thought life should be joyful, inspired, and full of possibility. That they should awaken with enthusiasm and energy for each new day. Something is not right. There is no real understanding of what is wrong. Just an uneasiness, a sadness, an overwhelm, or a dissatisfaction.

What is it? This discontent, desire for something different, or something more. When it first comes we deny it. It cannot be. I have everything I need. There is nothing really wrong with the life I am living. Why am I feeling this dissatisfaction, this longing, and this deep profound sadness? What can I do? Where can I turn? Who can I talk to? Who will understand? People will think I am crazy, feeling entitled, ungrateful, or not taking my responsibilities seriously.

Then one day after a sleepless night you awake exhausted. You know there is a better way. You know you will find help. Many have gone before you and practiced self-reliance or turned to God or source for help. You realize you're much stronger than you have been thinking. You get a journal and start to write. You remember you once heard it said, "We write to learn what we know and what we need to learn." You begin a long conversation with yourself, or the universe, asking questions, and as the answers come, you ask more.

The writing becomes easy and enlightening. Then it undulates, as do all human experiences and becomes painful, slow, and stagnant but you push on. You decide to find out what other writers have said. You start reading books. They pile high beside your bed. They impart their wisdom. You learn and grow.

Your experience of life changes. You wander through your heart and through the dark recesses of your mind. You realize that others have walked this path before. Becoming! Becoming who you are meant to be. Throwing off the "Thou shalt's!" and embracing the "What ifs?" Your days become filled with excitement, enthusiasm, and energy. The stagnation passes. You see a different view emerging – one you feel good about, are grateful for, and that pulls you on. Time passes and you embrace courage. This newfound bravery helps you overcome the fear and anxiety about standing out instead of hiding – about speaking your truth and beginning to walk your path. For a while you just slow down. You stop so much doing, and start to spend more time being. Being with yourself, being in nature, being in silence, and occasionally being with someone of like mind. Then you feel it growing deep inside, a quickening, and a change. You are emerging! Becoming is not easy. It's like giving birth. Giving birth to your new self. You feel a surge of joy and then undulate. Is this okay? Am I safe? Will I crash and burn? Who do I think I am? You dig yourself a deep hole filled with past limitations.

Eventually, you find the trail out. Eyes bright with wonder, you wander until you come across an idea to pursue. Maybe I could do this? You allow yourself to be vulnerable. You decide to do it. You encourage yourself to speak up – to be seen and heard. You are about to emerge when you stop! What am I doing? How did I get myself into this?

Fear and anxiety come and go like waves of the ocean. Yes, fear can affect even the best and most prolific of us. In the end we are all human, thank goodness, with all our emotions – fear, joy, worry, excitement, frustration – and we *react* until we remember to take that amazing deep breath, let it out slowly, and *respond* with consciousness.

It is then we move our nervous system from sympathetic to parasympathetic and regain what control we can. What is the worst thing that could happen? The world is still okay and so am I. As we breathe, more and more, our body warms. A smile fills our eyes and spreads across our face. We knew we could do it: but first we needed just a moment of massive insecurity. Now we are back stronger than ever. We don't just build strength in the gym. We build it every time we face fear and put it back in its place. And, as we become stronger and stronger we can eventually embrace bravery and live from our heart – the seat of love and courage.

We did not come to this planet to play small. We came to remember, learn, grow, and embrace our best possible selves. We see many today skirting the issue. They turn to alcohol, drugs, overconsumption of things and food. They vacillate between self-deprecation and self-aggrandizement. Or they attack others to prove how strong they are. Those that hurt others are hurting deep inside. They don't know how to release their pain. They fail to notice or realize the great power that is already in them – the "power to…" do what they choose to do.

If they would just go within and listen to that still small voice, and then with love *and hopefully help from another caring person who understands,* heal their traumatic pain and forgive themselves and others. We all need attention, affection, appreciation, and acceptance. We can give it to ourselves or to others. It is when we have a sense of belonging that we might find our gentle strength, compassion, caring, courage, and bravery. Fear leads to aggression and pain. Release the fear and you can be you – the you that is at your core – the one that came to this planet to live, love, speak truth passionately, laugh joyfully, and help others learn to live with love and bravery.

All any of us want is to belong, to be acknowledged, to be seen, to be appreciated, respected, and cared for. Can we do that for ourselves? Can we do that for each other? Can we heal our childhood or adult wounds? Can we open our hearts and be courageous enough to feel, and then through forgiveness heal our own pain? There will never be a better time than now. Now is the only time we have. We cannot allow ourselves to be divided into *us* and *them* and be manipulated to overlook another's pain and see only their hatred. It is time to let Darwin's "survival of the fittest" idea go and to embrace a new model of *survival of the most compassionate, caring, and kind.*

The history of humanity has been humans fighting humans for far too long. So many of us want peace. To paraphrase the Tao, *For there to be peace in the world, there must be peace in the country. For there to be peace in the country there must be peace in the home. For there to be peace in the home there must be peace in the heart.*

Fear is a heavy taskmaster. Fear leads to our destruction. Look around. Is it fear or love causing all the pain in the world? Fear spreads much faster than any virus. I remember the message from my favorite song, "You hold the key to love and fear right in your trembling hand. Just one key unlocks them both. It's at your command." Which will you choose? Choose love and heal yourself and the world.

We are on this planet to learn. Have we learned anything? Are we learning now? It is time to awaken to our magnificence and change our ways. So many of us desire change for the better. How can we convince others that there is no need for brutality, poverty, aggression, and pain? Love one another. Our future depends on it. Killing and destroying never has been a solution. Nobody ever wins a war. Peacefully and effectively standing for what we feel in the deepest corner of our heart will bring us the most strength and joy. As the Beetles sang, "All we need is love!" Making a difference for one other person is so very worth it. "Why am I trying so hard to fit in when I was meant to stand out?" We are on this precious planet together to learn, share, love ourselves, love others, shine brightly, and thrive.

It is time for us to shine. "We are the ones we have been waiting for." We are brilliant, brave and powerful. I am reminded of the song I used to sing. "Alone I can be a candle, a light for the world to see. But together we're a sun, shining light through eternity." May we lead with our hearts, find support from our source, fill this world with our brilliance, and in many small and profound ways edge out the darkness.

Lights in the Darkness

Inspirational quotes from Giants, named and unnamed

"If there is to be peace in the world,
There must be peace in the nations.
If there is to be peace in the nations,
There must be peace in the cities.
If there is to be peace in the cities,
There must be peace between neighbors.
If there is to be peace between neighbors,
There must be peace in the home.
If there is to be peace in the home,
There must be peace in the heart." Lao-tse

"So the sun was able to achieve by warmth and gentleness what the north wind in all his strength and furry could not do." Fable by La Fontaine used by Brian Wildsmith in *The North Wind and the Sun.*

To the whales the Wockatoo replied, "I have made you the strongest of all my creatures as a lesson that strength and gentleness can go hand in hand. Let us hope that others will learn this lesson from you." *Legend of the Whale*

"One generation plants the trees, and another gets the shade." Chinese Proverb

"My barn having burned down, I can now see the moon." Mitzuta Masahide, Samurai Poet

"Set your course by the stars, not by the lights of every passing ship." Omar N. Bradley

"Some men see things as they are and say why. I dream things that never were and say, why not?" Robert Kennedy

"Who am I trying to please at the expense of my joy?" Unknown

"If you keep a clear vision of your future, it will pull you like a magnet through your toughest times." Tony Robbins

"I am realistic. I expect miracles." Wayne Dyer

"If I have seen further, it is by standing on the shoulders of giants." Isaac Newton

"See a relationship as a place to give." Unknown

"For it is in giving that we receive." St. Francis of Assisi

"We don't see things as they are. We see them as we are." Anais Nin

"God, make me a hollow reed through which thy love can flow to others." Baha'i Song

"You never change things by fighting the existing reality. To change something, build a new model that makes the existing model obsolete." Buckminster Fuller

"Without goals, and plans to reach them, you are like a ship that has set sail with no destination." Fitzhugh Dodson

"A ship in port is safe, but that's not what ships are built for.' Grace Hooper

"I can be changed by what happena to me. But I refuse to be reduced by it." Maya Angelou

"There is no way to love. Love is the way,
There is no way to happiness. Happiness is the way,
There is no way to peace. Peace is the way." Dan Millman

The Guest House by Rumi

"Each person is a Guest House
Each morning a new arrival
A joy, depression, meanness
As an unexpected visitor
Welcome and entertain them all
Even if they are a crown of sorrows
Who violently sweep your house clean of furniture
Still treat each guest honorably
He may be clearing you out for some new delight
The dark thought, the shame, the malice
Meet them all at the door laughing and invite them in
Be grateful for whoever comes because
Each has been sent as a gentle guide from beyond."
Rumi

"Oh God, guide me and protect me
Illumine the lamp of my heart
And make of me a brilliant star
Thou art the Almighty and the powerful." Baha'i Prayer

"Your beliefs become your thoughts,
Your thoughts become your words,
You're words become your actions,
Your actions become your habits,
Your habits become your values,
Your values become your destiny." Gandhi

"Encountering adversity ultimately deepens us
and gives us access to our inner strength." Eckhart Tolle

"It's not too late
You're not too old.
You don't need to lose weight.
Your hair is fine.
Yes you can.
The fairytales were wrong.
No one is coming to save you.
If you don't go after what you want,
No one is going to waltz in
and hand it to you.
So go on now,
it's time you had your own
happily ever after."
Erin Matlock

Guiding Lights

"How many a man has dated a new era of his life from the reading of a book."
Henry David Thoreau

Books, DVD's, Podcasts

James Allen, *As a Man Thinketh*
Nancy Appleton, *Lick the Sugar Habit*
James F. Balch & Phyllis A. Balch, *Prescription for Nutritional Healing*
Byrd Baylor, *I'm in Charge of Celebrations*
Herbert Benson, *The Relaxation Response*
Joan Borysenko, *Minding the Body, Mending the Mind*
Gregg Braden, *The Divine Matrix, Human by Design, Fractal Time*
Kelly Brogan, *A Mind of Your Own, Own Yourself*
Brené Brown, *Dare to Lead, Braving the Wilderness*
Julia Cameron, *The Artist's Way*
Jack Canfield, *Chicken Soup for the Soul of Hawaii*
Mariana Caplan, *Yoga and Psyche: Integrating Paths of Yoga and Psychotherapy for Healing, Transformation, and Joy*
Deepak Chopra, *The Seven Laws of Spiritual Success, Perfect Health*
Deepak Chopra and David Simon, *The Seven Spiritual Laws of Yoga*

Kenneth S. Cohen, *The Way of Qigong*
Joe Dispenza, *Overcoming the Habit of Being Yourself, You Are the Placebo*
Ram Dass, *Be Here Now*
Sury Ram Das, *Awakening the Buddha Within: Tibetan Wisdom for the Western World*
William Dufty, *Sugar Blues*
Wayne Dyer, *The Power of Awakening*
Buckminster Fuller, *Operating Manual for Spaceship Earth*
Louise Hay, *You Can Heal Your Life*
Benjamin Hoff, *The Tao of Pooh*
Jean Houston, *Passion for the Possible*
Barbara Marx Hubbard, *Emergence: From Ego to Essence* – first edition
Sayer Ji, *Regenerate: Unlocking Your Body's Radical Resilience Through The New Biology*
Ted J. Kaptchuk, *The Web That Has No Weaver: Understanding Chinese Medicine*
Nicky Kassapian, *Be Yourself: The Art of Stepping Up*
Anne Morrow Lindbergh, *A Gift From the Sea*
Carolyn Myss, *Anatomy of Spirit*
Bruce Lipton, *Biology of Belief*
Bruce Lipton & Steve Bhaerman, *Spontaneous Evolution*
Lynn McTaggert, *The Field*
Anita Moorjani, *Dying To Be Me*
Byron Katie, *Loving What Is: Four Questions That Can Change Your Life*
Jack Kornfield, *A Path With Heart*
Erin Matlock, *Worth It*
John Perkins, *Touching the Jaguar: Transforming Fear into Action to Change Your Life and the World*
Steven G. Pratt and Kathy Matthews, *Super Foods, Super Foods Health Style*
Stephen Pressfield, *The Artist Journey*

Ken Robinson, *Finding Your Element*
Martin L. Rossman, *Guided Imagery for Self-Healing*
Jamie Samms, *Sacred Path Cards*
Anji Sandage and Lorena Novak Bull, *Everything Coconut Diet Cookbook*
Inna Segal, *The Secret Language of the Body*
Julie Shafer, *Loved: Relationship Rules for Women Who Thought They Knew the Rules*
Patanjuli, *Yoga Sutras of Patanjuli*, translation by Alistair Shearer
Michael Singer, *The Surrender Experiment, The Untethered Soul*
Ian Stansfield, *The Legend of the Whale*
Diane Stein, *Essential Reiki: A Complete Guide to an Ancient Healing Art*
Eckhart Tolle, *The Power of Now*
Lynn Twist, *The Soul of Money: Transforming Your Relationship With Money and Life*
Lao Tzu, *Tao Te Ching*, translation by Stephen Mitchell
Neal Donald Walsch, *Conversations with God*
Bradley J. Wilcox, D. Craig Wilcox, and Makato Suzuki, *The Okinawa Program: How the Worlds Longest Lived People Achieve Everlasting Health and How You Can Too*
Brian Wildsmith & La Fontaine, *The North Wind & the Sun: A Fable*
Robert M Williams, *The Missing Piece/Peace In Your Life*
Marianne Williamson, *The Law of Divine Compensation: On Work, Money, and Miracles*
Gary Zukav, *The Seat of the Soul*

Podcasts

At the End of the Tunnel, Light Watkins
Unlocking Us, Brené Brown
The One You Feed, Eric Zimmer
Inspiration Nation, Michael Sandler
Broken Brain, Dhru Purohit
Seeds, Steven Moe from New Zealand

Videos

Many of the authors listed in this book have videos on YouTube.
Serenity Retreat Season, Patti Ernst & Melissa Flagg www.serenitybeaches.com
Michael Singer, many YouTube videos
I Am, Tom Shadyak
Foster Gambel and Kimberly Carter Gambel, *Thrive and Thrive II*

About the Author

Patti Ernst is an explorer, adventurer, learner, and risk taker. When she was young she dreamed of these things but it was not until her forties that she started her explorations, and in her fifties, her adventures. She has spent time in the cities and backcountry of China, Venezuela, Guatemala, Ecuador, Mexico, Puerto Rico, Thailand, Papua New Guinea, Indonesia, Japan, Australia, New Zealand, Europe, Eastern Europe, and the South Pacific islands. In her sixties she sailed for two and a half years and then built a resort in the South Pacific.

Patti has a master's degree in education, is a Chopra certified Perfect Health instructor, a Reiki Master, a yoga and meditation teacher. As a massage therapist she worked at the Four Seasons on the Big Island of Hawaii. Her focus is on helping herself and others keep body/mind/spirit functioning optimally so that life on this planet can be a joyful adventure. When she left her home in upstate New York she had been a wife, mother, and teacher for over thirty-five years. At fifty-six she realized it was time to move forward, discover her passion, and live her purpose in life.

This workbook is about processes it was necessary for her to go through on her journey. As she continues to grow she continues to find more inspiration. This book is not a prescription, but a record of the ideas that she explored and areas you might wish to consider to gain a greater understanding of awareness and self-care and to create your path forward.

As a child she was shy, well behaved, and a people-pleaser. As a wife and mother she loved her family and enjoyed their life style, but did what she was expected to do. She kept feeling that when she turned forty she would give herself permission to be her true self, but that decade came and went and she was still doing what was expected of her. It was in her fifties that she energetically began opening to possibilities.

She read books that stretched her awareness, started asking questions, and began to travel. It was a long process. She moved to Alaska, then to Hawaii, sailed for two and a half years, and built a resort in Tonga, which she still runs. Today others often awaken at a much younger age. There are more people choosing to express who they truly are, writing books, acting as guides, and creating podcasts and videos. Change is still a difficult task. That is why she offers this book, a companion to her first book *Journey to Serenity*, as a source of information, guidance, and possibilities.

www.serenitybeaches.com

www.ingramcontent.com/pod-product-compliance
Lightning Source LLC
Chambersburg PA
CBHW031114080526
44587CB00011B/963